SEA RAIDERS OF THE AMERICAN REVOLUTION

THE CONTINENTAL NAVY IN EUROPEAN WATERS

E. Gordon Bowen-Hassell
Dennis M. Conrad
and
Mark L. Hayes

NAVAL HISTORICAL CENTER
DEPARTMENT OF THE NAVY
WASHINGTON
2003

Secretary of the Navy's
Advisory Subcommittee on Naval History

Library of Congress Cataloging-in-Publication Data
Bowen-Hassell, E. Gordon, 1940-
    Sea raiders of the American Revolution : the Continental Navy in European waters /
E. Gordon Bowen-Hassell, Dennis M. Conrad, and Mark L. Hayes
        p. cm.
    Includes bibliographical references.
    ISBN 0-945274-49-1 (pbk. : alk. paper)
    1. Wickes, Lambert, 1742?-1777. Conyngham, Gustavus, 1744?-1819. 3. Jones,
John Paul, 1747-1792. 4. Sailors--United States--Biography. 5. Admirals--United
States--Biography. 6. United States. Continental Navy--Biography. 7. United States--
History--Revolution, 1775-1783--Naval operations. 8. United States--Foreign relations-
-1775-1783. 9. United States--Foreign relations--Europe. 10. Europe--Foreign rela-
tions--United States. I. Conrad, Dennis Michael, 1949- II. Hayes, Mark L. III. Title.

E206.B69 2003
973.3'5'0922--dc21   2003046467
[B]

For sale by the Superintendent of Documents, U.S. Government Printing Office
Internet: bookstore.gpo.gov – Phone: 202-512-1800 – Fax: 202-512-2250 –
Mail: Superintendent of Documents, Mail Stop SSOP, Washington, DC 20402-9328

I was early and have ever been of the opinion that under God our salvation must finally come from vigorous and bold operations at sea, and by carrying the war to their commerce, and factories in distant quarters of the globe.

—Silas Deane to Jonathan Trumbull, 23 May 1777

It appears to me to be the province of our Infant Navy to Surprise and spread Alarms with fast Sailing Ships,—when we grow stronger we can mcct their Fleets and dispute with them the Sovereignty of the Ocean.

—John Paul Jones to Benjamin Franklin, 1 June 1778

Contents

Foreword

The United States Navy is defined by its history, a shared heritage binding the disparate parts of the American naval community and connecting today's Sailors with those who manned the fleet two hundred years ago. The service's mores and rules of conduct stand solidly on the foundation of the Navy's illustrious past. This booklet, one in an occasional series, brings our naval heritage into the light once again so that all can learn from it.

The Naval Historical Center strives to acquaint today's Sailors with those who have gone before because a widespread knowledge of this history enhances the fleet's effectiveness, while familiarity with the Navy's heritage strengthens each Sailor's pride in the service. In the rush and pressure of everyday duties and deadlines, naval personnel may set aside the task of looking at history for leisure time, assuming nothing practical for the workday can be gleaned from studying the careers of captains who commanded ships powered by sails and armed with smooth-bore cannon. Those who make this assumption and neglect history make a mistake. Intangibles like leadership, teamwork, and commitment hold timeless lessons unconnected to technology. Looking at how a naval captain in the American Revolution exercised command can provide today's Sailors at all levels with a blueprint for leadership and an understanding of what worked and what did not.

Finally, the travails and triumphs of our naval forebears inspire us and prepare us to meet our own crises. Let us look to those earlier American naval leaders who faced long odds and seemingly invincible foes, sometimes overcoming them, sometimes falling before them, but always meeting them with courage. From their example, let us draw strength to confront our enemies in these dangerous times.

William S. Dudley
Director of Naval History

Preface

The Navy of the United States, like the nation itself, was born in the midst of the bloody conflict for independence known as the American Revolution. The Continental Navy, as it was called then, shaped and was shaped by this difficult struggle for freedom that lasted from 1775 to 1783. During the war, the sailors of the young navy, seamen and officers alike, established the proud traditions of honor, courage, and commitment shared by today's servicemen in the United States Navy. It is important for the American people, especially those who wear the uniform, to understand the significant role that the Continental Navy played in the nation's beginnings.

This book is about three captains of the Continental Navy: Lambert Wickes, Gustavus Conyngham, and John Paul Jones. In recounting the stories of their lives and examining the roles they played in the Navy's early years, it highlights the difficult circumstances that each man faced operating in seas dominated by the British Navy and emphasizes that the outcome of the American War for Independence was far from certain. The book also illustrates the humanity of these Revolutionary War heroes, revealing their weaknesses as well as their strengths. They exhibited frustration, pettiness, and egotism as well as courage, initiative, and sound judg-ment. Like naval leaders today, these Continental Navy officers faced tough choices and were forced to live with the consequences, for good or ill. Their lives and choices had an important influence on the course of the war and on the character of the naval service.

We, the authors, are historians in the Early History Branch of the Naval Historical Center located at the Washington Navy Yard. Our branch serves the Navy by presenting its history from the American Revolution through World War I. In fulfilling that responsibility we help edit a multi-volume publication called *Naval Documents of the American Revolution,* which consists of transcriptions of original documents concerning the naval history of the American Revolution. The expertise that we have gained from working on that project has helped us to write this booklet.

The interpretations expressed herein are those of the authors alone, as are any errors of fact or interpretation.

E. Gordon Bowen-Hassell
Dennis M. Conrad
Mark L. Hayes

Introduction

By the autumn of 1775, the British North American colonies from Maine to Georgia were in open rebellion. Royal governments had been thrown out of many colonial capitals and revolutionary governments put in their places. The Continental Congress in Philadelphia had assumed some of the responsibilities of a central government for the colonies, created a Continental Army, issued paper money for the support of the troops, and formed a committee to negotiate with foreign countries. Continental forces captured Fort Ticonderoga on Lake Champlain and launched an invasion of Canada. The Revolutionaries had yet to work out whether they were fighting for their rights as British subjects or for their rights as citizens of an independent nation. They also had to decide whether they would need a navy to help win those rights.

Birth of the Continental Navy

In October 1775 the British dominated the seas and threatened to block the colonists' trade and to wreak destruction on their coastal settlements. In response a few of the revolutionary governments had commissioned small fleets of their own for defense of local waters. Some in Congress, hoping that reconciliation with the mother country was still possible, worried that American naval operations might push the armed struggle too far. Others from the outset of armed hostilities had advocated a Continental Navy. They argued that a national navy would defend seaports, protect vital trade, retaliate against British raiders, and make it possible to seek out from among neutral nations of the world the arms and stores necessary for resistance.

On Friday, October 13, 1775, matters came to a head and the advocates for a navy won the argument. Congress voted to fit out two sailing vessels armed with ten cannon each, as well as other arms, and manned by crews of eighty and to send them on a three-month cruise to intercept transports carrying munitions and supplies to the British army in America. This legislation, out of which the Continental Navy grew, constitutes the birth certificate of today's Navy.

Within a few days of its first resolution to employ armed vessels, Congress established a Naval Committee charged with equipping a fleet. This committee directed the purchasing, outfitting, manning, and operations of the first ships of the new Navy, drafted subsequent naval legislation, and prepared rules and regulations to govern the Continental Navy's conduct and internal administration.

During the War of Independence, no suitable alternative to a national navy was available to serve the purposes of Congress. Wherever there were military objectives requiring naval support, public vessels commanded by commissioned officers, subject to the will of the Continental Congress, were essential to carrying out the mission.

Forward Deployment and Foreign Relations

If Continental Navy vessels were to operate in European waters, where they could bring the war home to the British enemy, their commanders would have to find European powers willing to allow them to use their ports. A logical candidate was France, a long-time rival of England. France, however, had agreed by treaty neither to allow the cruisers or prizes of Great Britain's enemies to enter its ports, nor to permit those cruisers to fit out in its territory. Despite these treaty obligations, France decided to give American warships all possible aid while pretending to remain neutral. American commanders found that it was generally possible to dispose of prizes and obtain refits, supplies, and seamen in French ports. The only effective way the British could deny Americans the use of French ports was to blockade them, an action that would have started an undesired war with France.

The French enjoyed seeing Great Britain's North American colonies in revolt. With their conquest of Canada in the Seven Years' War in 1763, the British had driven the French out of North America. French leaders believed that Great Britain's economic prowess, based on colonial trade, gave the British disproportionate influence in international affairs. By supporting the American revolt, the French hoped to redress the balance of power in Europe. Indeed, a major impulse for Congress to adopt the Declaration of Independence in July 1776 was to persuade France to come to America's aid by making America's reconciliation with the mother country less likely.

Besides allowing American cruisers use of their ports, the French gave the United States grants and loans of money for purchasing war supplies. France had secretly supplied the Continental Army shiploads of munitions and uniforms by the time King Louis XVI signed formal treaties of friendship and commerce and of alliance in February 1778. Soon thereafter, France threw off the mask of neutrality and joined in the war in support of the United States. The French navy's substantial contributions to the winning of American independence culminated in the Battle off the Virginia Capes, which led to the capture of a British army besieged by combined Continental and French forces at Yorktown in 1781 and the successful end to the war.

American cruisers also found a welcome in the ports of Spain, whose king, Charles III, sought, as did his French relative Louis XVI, to humble Great Britain by giving secret aid to the American revolutionaries. He was reluctant, however, to recognize the independence of the revolting British colonies because he feared encouraging independence movements among Spain's own American colonies. Urged on by France, Charles III entered the war against Great Britain in 1779, hoping for territorial gains, in particular for the reconquest of Gibraltar. Spain, however, did not enter into an alliance with the United States.

Three Continental Navy Captains in Europe

The three Continental Navy captains whose stories are found in the following chapters followed one another into European waters. Although each brought the war home to the enemy by raiding in British waters, each possessed a different vision of what he wanted to accomplish, and each made a significant contribution to the winning of American independence.

Lambert Wickes led the way. As the trailblazer, he was the one who tested the possibilities of using French ports as bases for commerce raiding cruises,

devised practical ways around legal and bureaucratic obstacles, and developed the model for disposing of captured ships. Wickes' main strategic goal was to embroil France and Great Britain in diplomatic disputes that would result in war between them.

Gustavus Conyngham concentrated on cruising against British commerce. He and other American commerce raiders forced the British Admiralty to assign additional Royal Navy vessels to convoy duty, thus lessening the number of vessels available to enforce a blockade of the North American coast. The loss of ships to these raids increased the desire for peace among the British merchant community.

John Paul Jones cared little about commerce raiding for its own sake, viewing it principally as a means of obtaining the funds needed to sustain his operations, as well as of capturing British prisoners to use in exchange for captive American sailors. He sought primarily to make the British feel the evils of the war they had brought to the shores of America. Therefore, he not only attacked their shipping but also raided their shores.

As different as Wickes, Conyngham, and Jones were from each other, they were representative of many others who served under their country's flag in command of Continental Navy vessels. Over the course of the Revolutionary War, the Continental Navy sent more than fifty armed vessels to sea. American squadrons and cruisers seized enemy supplies, carried correspondence and diplomats to Europe, and transported munitions to America. They also convoyed coin needed to pay the Continental Army and prevent army mutiny. In addition, Continental Navy commanders captured nearly two hundred vessels as prizes, some off the British Isles themselves, contributing to the demoralization of the enemy and forcing the Royal Navy to divert warships to protect convoys and trade routes. In addition, American naval operations provoked diplomatic crises that helped bring France into the war against Great Britain. The Continental Navy and its valiant captains began the proud heritage and tradition celebrated by our United States Navy today.

Michael J. Crawford
Head, Early History Branch
Naval Historical Center

Lambert Wickes

By E. Gordon Bowen-Hassell

ambert Wickes, one of the more audacious and courageous captains in the Navy of the United States (known as the Continental Navy from 1775 to 1783), is today remembered by only a handful of Revolutionary War naval historians and history buffs. One reason is that Wickes' naval career was short. He died early in the American Revolution when his ship sank while returning to America after a series of triumphs in British waters. But it is perhaps his modesty, more than the shortness of his career, that shrouds this captain in mystery. This anonymity is undeserved and sailors of the United States Navy, officers and enlisted, should know of Lambert Wickes and of his exploits, for he was a hero and a trailblazer whose accomplishments helped establish the Navy's proud heritage.

Early Life

The second son of Samuel Wickes, Lambert was born about 1742 on Eastern Neck Island in Kent County, Maryland. Wickes was a member of a prominent family whose roots in America date back to 1650. Nothing is known of his physical appearance, as no portraits or contemporary descriptions of him have survived.

Like so many men from the Eastern Shore, Wickes felt drawn to a seafaring life. Customs records for the ports of Maryland reveal that by the age of eighteen Wickes was an accomplished enough mariner to command his own ship.

Well before colonial opposition to taxes imposed by the British Parliament led to the open warfare of the American Revolution, Lambert Wickes proved his loyalty to American ideals and earned the gratitude and respect of his fellow Marylanders. In the fall of 1774, irate citizens of Annapolis, Maryland, observed a "tea party" more dramatic than the famous Boston Tea Party, by forcing the owners of the merchant ship *Peggy Stewart* to burn the ship. London merchants had sent the offending vessel with tea from England in defiance of non-importation resolutions, adopted to protest the hated Parliamentary tax on tea. The same merchants pressured Wickes to import a consignment of tea in the ship *Neptune*, of which he was master and part owner. Two weeks after the burning of *Peggy*

Stewart, Wickes returned to Annapolis from London. In a deposition given before the Committee of Observation of Anne Arundel County, Wickes declared that he had fought attempts to ship tea in *Neptune*, "having formed a resolution not to carry any tea to America," even if it meant taking a financial loss by sailing home without a cargo. Wickes received the committee's thanks for his patriotic conduct.

Appointment as Captain in the Continental Navy

The Revolutionary War began the following spring, with the Battles of Lexington and Concord. In June 1775, the Continental Congress appointed George Washington commander in chief of the newly formed Continental Army, and that fall, it established a Continental Navy to carry the war for American rights onto the sea. When it came time to appoint officers for the new navy, Revolutionary leaders, including Robert Morris, vice president of the Continental Marine Committee, and Matthew Tilghman, Maryland delegate to the Continental Congress, remembered the patriotism of Captain Lambert Wickes of Maryland and, in April 1776, commissioned him a naval captain. In the official ranking of Continental Navy captains of 10 October 1776, the Marine Committee ranked Wickes as number eleven.

At the time of Wickes' appointment, John Barry, commanding the Continental Navy brigantine *Lexington*, operated out of Philadelphia, running the British blockade of the Delaware River to make short cruises. Morris urged Congress to purchase another vessel to assist Barry in providing protection for American shipping in Delaware Bay. Congress promptly complied by purchasing a former merchant ship, *Molly*, then lying at Philadelphia. *Molly*, now renamed *Reprisal*, was a full-rigged ship of about 200 tons with tall masts for royals. It was about one hundred feet long and thirty feet wide. The ship had a female figurehead, black sides with white molding around the quarters, and a yellow and black stern. It carried eighteen 6-pounder carriage guns and was served by a crew of 130 seamen. The Marine Committee appointed Wickes to command *Reprisal*.

The new Continental Navy captain had to surmount a number of obstacles in following his orders to fit out *Reprisal* "with all possible expedition." Philadelphia's shipyards were overburdened with building four frigates and refitting and repairing *Hornet* and *Lexington*, all for the Continental Navy, while Philadelphians had begun to fit out privateers, drawing away potential recruits from the navy. It testifies to Wickes' leadership and perseverance that he completed *Reprisal*'s conversion to a warship and mustered its entire crew by 28 April, when it set sail from Philadelphia for convoy duty in Delaware River and Bay.

Battle with British Frigates in the Delaware River

Lambert Wickes first saw action against the Royal Navy in early May 1776, after word reached Philadelphia that H.M. frigates *Roebuck* and *Liverpool* were sailing up the Delaware River in pursuit of Continental Navy schooner *Wasp*, Captain Charles Alexander, commander. In this pursuit, *Roebuck* ran aground off Wilmington, and the Pennsylvania State Navy fleet under Captain Thomas Read dropped down the river to check the British advance. The Continental Marine Committee ordered Wickes to accompany the flagship of the state fleet, *Montgomery*, to assist in challenging the British frigates. On 7 May Captain Read requested Wickes to provide seamen to help man two pilot boats and two small fire sloops, in accordance with orders from the Marine Committee to supply men to the Pennsylvania Navy.

Read's report affords a brief insight into Wickes' thinking. Because the Marine Committee's instructions had not yet reached Wickes, he replied to Read, "I have received no order from the Marine Committee and I cannot let any of my men go without one. I wish that I could and I will immediately upon receipt of the order." This measured response indicates that

William Bingham, Continental agent at Martinique; Wickes transported him to that post.

Wickes at the very start of his career understood the first requisite of a naval officer—to follow the commands of his superiors in his department only. As soon as he received his orders, Wickes complied. He sent the first lieutenant of *Reprisal*, Lieutenant Robert Harris, and ten sailors to the fire sloops and dispatched Captain of Marines Miles Pennington with two sergeants and twenty-four Continental Marines to the pilot boats. After two furious long-range gun battles on May 8 and May 9 with the Pennsylvania Navy galleys, *Roebuck* freed itself and with *Liverpool* fell down the Delaware to make much needed repairs to sails and rigging.

In Cape May Channel

During the rest of May, *Reprisal* with three other Continental Navy vessels— brigantine *Lexington*, Captain John Barry, sloop *Hornet*, Captain William Hallock, and schooner *Wasp*, Captain Charles Alexander—convoyed merchant ships down Delaware Bay and cruised off the Delaware Capes to protect inward-bound American vessels from British frigates.

Tiring of this duty, Wickes wrote the Continental Marine Committee on 6 June soliciting an opportunity to make an independent cruise. The Marine Committee granted the Marylander's wish on 10 June when it directed him to sail on a diplomatic mission under the orders of the Continental Committee of Secret Correspondence (later, the Foreign Affairs Committee). The committee directed Wickes to embark William Bingham and convey him to his important post as Continental Agent on the French West Indian island of Martinique. Before departing Martinique, Wickes was to lay in a store of muskets and munitions for the Continental Army. Bingham arrived in *Wasp* on 13 June in the Cape May Channel and promptly boarded *Reprisal* with the committee's orders. Wickes enthusiastically replied on 16 June to the Committee of Secret Correspondence: "You may depend on my best

LE FORT St PIERRE DANS   L'ISLE DE LA MARTINIQUE

Vu du   Mouillage.

Tiré d'un Receuil de differents Ports   *des Isles Antilles dessinés en 1780*

Réunis à la Collection des Ports   *de France, gravés par le Sr Gouaz.*

A Paris chez le Gouaz Graveur rue St Hyacinte la 1re porte a gauche par la place St Michel.

Saint-Pierre Roadstead, Martinique, site of engagement between Reprisal *and HM sloop* Shark.

endeavours in your Service to prosecute this Voyage with the Most expedition and Advantage in my power." He added: "my People . . . are in good health, & the Officers are well Satisfied with this Cruize, hopeing thereby to Render their Country an Assential Service."

While Wickes waited for the British frigates cruising off the Delaware Capes to leave or be driven off station by a change in wind, which would give *Reprisal* an opportunity to slip out to sea, he was involved in a bloody action between American and British naval forces off Cape May. On 28 June the American merchant brig *Nancy* was returning from the Danish islands of St. Croix and St. Thomas with a valuable cargo of gunpowder, muskets, and rum, when H.M. frigate *Orpheus* and H.M. sloop *Kingfisher* sighted and chased it northwards from Cape May. Observing the chase, the Continental Navy vessels hoisted out their ship's boats and sent them under the command of the senior officer present, Captain John Barry, to *Nancy's* rescue in Turtle Gut Inlet, N.J. Wickes' younger brother, Lieutenant Richard Wickes, *Reprisal's* third lieutenant, was at the helm of the *Reprisal's* barge, and another early naval hero, then-lieutenant Joshua Barney, steered a barge from *Wasp*. In order to save the brig's cargo Barry determined to run the merchantman hard aground on a shoal offshore and transfer the munitions in boats to the beach. The Americans took off about two hundred barrels of gunpowder and fifty muskets before enemy gunfire compelled them to abandon *Nancy*. Before quitting the brig, they laid a train of powder, which blew up as the British boarding party from *Kingfisher* stepped on board.

Lieutenant Richard Wickes played a conspicuous role in removing the barrels of gunpowder to the shore. Sadly, a cannonball killed him near the end of the fight, passing through his arm and body. "We have this Consolation," Lambert Wickes wrote his elder brother Samuel, "that he fought like a brave Man & was fore most in every Transaction of that Day." As consoling as a heroic death might have been, it could not entirely alleviate the pain Wickes felt over Richard's death. As he told Samuel, "I have lost a dear Brother & a good officer."

Cruise to Martinique

Reprisal finally sailed from Cape May for Martinique on 3 July, escorting thirteen merchantmen to sea. Wickes reported elatedly on 11 July to the Committee of Secret Correspondence that *Reprisal* convoyed them "a good distance from the land" and "they all got safely off." Now on his own, Wickes learned the excellent sailing qualities of *Reprisal*. He whipped his crew into shape by drilling them at han-

LE FORT ROYAL DANS L'ISLE DE LA MARTINIQUE
Vu du Mouillage.
Tiré d'un Recueil de differens Ports des Isles Antilles defsinés en 1780,
Réunis à la Collection des Ports de France, gravés par le Sr. Gouaz.
A Paris chez le Gouaz Graveur, rue St. Hyacinte, la 1ere porte à gauche par la Place St. Michel

dling the sails and exercising them at the 6-pounder guns and small arms.

On this first cruise, Wickes displayed initiative, a quality requisite in all excellent naval officers. Even though he had an important diplomat on board his ship, he evidently did not judge that the Committee of Secret Correspondence's orders precluded the taking of prizes. Between 11 and 16 July, *Reprisal* captured three British merchantmen with valuable cargoes of sugar, rum, cocoa, and coffee, which Wickes sent to Philadelphia and New Jersey. To sail these prizes to their intended destinations, Wickes sent forty-three of his best seamen and master's mates, leaving him only eighty-seven trustworthy seamen in *Reprisal*. On the other hand, using the lure of prize money, he persuaded thirty-nine of his prisoners to enroll as members of the crew of *Reprisal*.

About 21 July near the northern tip of the Leeward Islands, *Reprisal* chased and stopped a fourth West Indiamen, *Dutchess of Leinster,* bound to Cork, but, because of his reduced crew, Wickes wisely decided to release the prize. Instead of giving the true reason for not taking the vessel, Wickes told the captain of the merchantman he would release this ship because it was Irish property and America was not at war with Ireland. Wickes employed diplomatic shrewdness by telling the master of the Irish ship "he would not distress him, because he was sure the Irish would not distress them." He clearly hoped the captain would carry these sentiments back to Ireland where they would be

Fort Royal Bay, Martinique, French naval base where Wickes cleaned and refitted Reprisal.

published in local newspapers, and in fact they were.

On 27 July *Reprisal* looked into Saint-Pierre roadstead, the principal seaport of Martinique, only to find H.M. sloop *Shark* (16 guns), Commander John Chapman, lying serenely at anchor. Judiciously deciding not to endanger Bingham's life in an action, Wickes ordered one of *Reprisal*'s boats lowered into the water with the Continental Agent and had him rowed to shore. Chapman soon spied the rakish black ship wearing "Colours which I was unacquainted with (being red & white striped with a Union next the Staff)." The stars and stripes flag not having been adopted as yet, *Reprisal* flew the Grand Union flag, consisting of the British Union Jack with the crosses of Saint George and Saint Andrew in the upper quarter next to the staff, and thirteen red and white horizontal stripes. *Shark* immediately got underway and stood out to speak the stranger at 7 PM. *Reprisal* continued on a southerly tack until 8:30 PM when it tacked and sailed westward to gain sea room.

Chapman repeatedly hailed *Reprisal*, and *Shark* fired a shot across the bow at 9 PM, whereupon *Reprisal* wore and bore down on *Shark*, firing a broadside into the sloop. A general engagement of three or four broadsides lasting for forty-five minutes ensued with little damage being inflicted by either side, although the British sloop took at least three hits. *Shark* sheered off to join its schooner tender but, being too close to the lower battery of Sainte-Marthe, received two warning shots from the Frenchmen and then stood out to sea. For his gallantry in the battle, Wickes gained the sympathy of the French commandant at St. Pierre and received a joyous reception from the Martinique populace, who had observed the action from the shore and appreciated watching a representative of the haughty British navy bested.

Wickes became the first Continental Navy captain to make a formal call on a European nation's official representative when he paid his respects to Baron de Courcy, commandant of the town and fort of St. Pierre. De Courcy granted Wickes' two requests, that *Reprisal* be protected while in port and that it be allowed to heave down to clean its bottom. By 1 August *Shark* had departed for Antigua. *Reprisal* then sailed down the coast to Fort Royal Bay, the French naval base at Martinique, where every facility was extended to the ship to heave down and refit. Although lionized by the inhabitants, the always-modest Wickes left the diplomatic and mercantile aspects of the mission to Bingham. Being a man of action, Wickes devoted his time to getting *Reprisal* refitted for its return voyage. *Reprisal* set sail from Fort Royal Bay on 26 August and anchored off Philadelphia on 13 September after an uneventful passage.

Before Lambert Wickes' arrival, Philadelphia newspapers had published accounts of his successes as each of his three prizes carrying letters from Martinique describing *Reprisal*'s engagement with *Shark* arrived safely in port. Wickes, therefore, received a hero's welcome. According to one newspaper, "Captain Wickes and his ship's crew have acquired much applause," and to another, "Captain Weeks behaved extremely well, and has acquired much honor and reputation with the French at Martinique." Perhaps the ultimate appreciation of Wickes' accomplishments on his first cruise came from Benjamin Franklin and Robert Morris who wrote: "Captain Wickes's behaviour meets with the approbation of his Country & Fortune seems to have had an Eye to his Merit when She Conducted

Benjamin Franklin, head of the American commissioners to France, whom Wickes transported across the Atlantic.

his three Prizes safely in."

On 14 September the Marylander began unloading *Reprisal*, and sent the muskets and gunpowder on to the beleaguered Continental Army in New Jersey.

Cruise to France

No sooner had Wickes finished unloading *Reprisal* at the wharf in Philadelphia than he received terse orders from the Continental Marine Committee to get *Reprisal* immediately fitted out and manned for a two-month cruise. The committee did not divulge the purpose or destination of this cruise. But on 11 October Congress instructed the Marine Committee "to deliver to the direction of the Committee of Secret Correspondence two of the Continental cruisers now ready for sea, to perform such voyages as they shall think necessary for the service of these states." On 23 October, on oral orders from the Marine Committee, Wickes sailed *Reprisal* down the Delaware River to Marcus Hook, just south of Chester, Pennsylvania, where he awaited further orders from the committee. The next day, the committee ordered him to place himself and *Reprisal* again under the direction of the Committee of Secret Correspondence, assuring the captain, "We hold you in Much esteem, and flatter ourselves your Conduct in the Service will always be such as to meet the Continuance of it."

On that same day, the Committee of Secret Correspondence dispelled the mystery of Wickes' new mission by issuing him orders to proceed in *Reprisal* to Nantes, France, conveying Benjamin Franklin to his post as one of the American commissioners in France. Wickes' orders emphasized a speedy and safe voyage; he was not to cruise for prizes or communicate with other vessels unless Franklin approved. On landing Franklin at Nantes, Wickes was to refit *Reprisal* in the Loire River in "two or three days" and sail immediately on a short cruise against enemy shipping in the English Channel, before the British could gain any knowledge of him. The committee even suggested he might take one of the English packets inward- or outward-bound from Falmouth, perhaps the Lisbon packet, which carried gold and silver coin. Any prisoners who would not sign on *Reprisal* Wickes was to put on shore in France, misleading them with the report that he was headed to St. Georges Channel in order to cruise for ships from Bristol. The committee also directed him to dispatch to America valuable prizes laden with cargoes that might be immediately wanted, such as woolens and linen goods. Other prizes might be sent to French ports after removing valuable goods into *Reprisal*.

The committee thought the French would be accommodating: "Docter Franklin will make application at the Court of France for the protection of Their ports to the *Reprisal* and her prizes, and we hope he will be Successfull." If the French proved unwilling to grant protection to *Reprisal* and its prizes, Wickes was to return to America. If the French granted the desired protection, he was to remain in France under the direction of the American commissioners.

One sentence in his orders concerning prize money

> "let Old England See how they like to have an active Enemy at their own Door, they have Sent Fire and Sword to ours."

must have caused Wickes concern: "The Congress will pay here [Philadelphia] yours and the peoples Shares of Such money, as well as their Shares of any prizes or parts of Prizes that may be Sold there [in France] and the Money applyed to publick use." This meant that no prize money was to be distributed to the crew of *Reprisal* in France and that any monies accruing from sales of prizes must be deposited in the expense account of the American commissioners in Paris. These provisions could leave the captain with few means to satisfy a crew displeased with having to wait to be paid money due them.

Lest the objective of cruising in British waters be misunderstood, the committee stated emphatically: "let Old England See how they like to have an active Enemy at their own Door, they have Sent Fire and Sword to ours." Finally, Lambert Wickes was reminded "A Spirited active conduct in this enterprize will recommend you to all America."

Benjamin Franklin and his two grandsons arrived at Marcus Hook in secret on 27 October and immediately boarded *Reprisal* for an eventful voyage. Although beset by gales and heavy seas for most of the crossing, *Reprisal* lived up to its reputation as a fast sailer, making a quick Atlantic passage. Departing from Cape Henlopen on 29 October, the ship reached France exactly one month later, making the *Reprisal* the first Continental Navy ship and Lambert Wickes the first Continental Navy captain to arrive in European waters.

On the morning of 27 November Wickes spied a sail and, evidently obtaining Franklin's permission to stop and search, sent his cutter to board the vessel. It proved to be the brigantine *George*, with thirty-five hogsheads of wine, staves, tar, and turpentine. Within a few hours *Reprisal* took a more valuable prize, the ship *Vine*, with a cargo of brandy and flaxseed. Thus Wickes scored another first, being the first Continental Navy captain to capture prizes in European waters. Perhaps Franklin decided the best way to test the French attitude toward American prizes was to send two of them into a French port, which is what Wickes did. Buffeted by strong head winds, *Reprisal* was unable to enter the Loire River and therefore sought shelter in Quiberon Bay on 29 November.

Franklin was most complimentary of Wickes' performance during the crossing: "Capt Wicks did every thing in his Power to make the Voyage comfortable to me; and I was much pleas'd with what I saw of his Conduct as an Officer, when on suppos'd Occasions we made Preparation for engagement, the good Order & Readiness with which it was done, being far beyond my expectation, and I believe equal to any thing of the kind in the best Ships in the King's fleet." As tokens of his thanks, he presented Wickes with forty-eight livres to be divided among the cabin boys and two casks of wine for the crew.

Waiting for a favorable wind, *Reprisal* remained at anchor in Quiberon Bay with the masters and crews of the two prizes on board. The wind continuing unfavorable, on 3 December Wickes obtained a fishing boat to put the impatient Franklin on shore at Auray, so he could set out overland for Nantes in order to determine what to do with the prizes.

Once Franklin got to Nantes on 7 December, he consulted with the prominent merchant house of Pliarne, Penet & Co. about the prizes and, in particular, huddled with its senior partner, Jacques Gruel, and the firm's American associate, Nathan Rumsey. Franklin dashed off a letter to the Committee of Secret Correspondence on 8 December reporting, "The Captains have made some Propositions of Ransom, which perhaps may be accepted." In another letter of the same date to the President of Congress, John Hancock, Franklin described the situation more fully: "There is some difficulty in determining what to do with them [the prizes], as they are scarce worth sending to America, and the mind of the French court with regard to prizes brought into their ports is not yet known. It is certainly contrary to their treaties with Britain to permit the sale of them, and we have no means of trying and condemning them. There are, however, many here who would purchase prizes we having already had several offers from persons who are willing to take upon themselves all consequences as to the illegallity."

Franklin sent Rumsey, who had already been approached by several prospective buyers, to Quiberon Bay to help Wickes with the sale of the prizes and cargos. On 13 December Wickes in his first letter from France to the Committee of Secret Correspondence stated, "I have no Doubt but we shall be allowed to sell our prizes here, as there has been 10 or a Dozen Merchants on board to purchase the two prizes, now in my possession." In the meantime he transferred twenty-two puncheons of brandy from *Vine* to *Reprisal* for the ship's use. Rumsey arrived about this time, and he and Wickes collaborated with great success. They

developed what became the standard method for Americans to dispose of prizes in French ports prior to the Franco-American alliance in 1778. Sales were conducted clandestinely at night or at sea just outside a major port. The purchaser, who would get the vessel at a bargain price, assumed all responsibility for any illegalities. The purchaser would change the vessel's name before bringing it into port and then register it in the port's records under false papers. A merchant at Auray bought *George,* and Rumsey purchased *Vine*. Together the two prizes netted only 39,600 livres (approximately £1,700), which was considerably less than the £4,000 that Wickes expected.

On the morning of 17 December the winds finally changed, and *Reprisal* weighed anchor and stood out of Quiberon Bay. In the evening it entered the estuary of the Loire, ascending the river as far as St. Nazaire. On the next day *Reprisal* sailed up the Loire and anchored off Paimboeuf, where Wickes released the masters and crews of the prizes.

In keeping with his orders from the Committee of Secret Correspondence, Wickes hastily refitted *Reprisal* for a short cruise, arranging only for a replenishment of fresh water and provisions. By 24 December Wickes was "ready to sail at half hour's warning," but in the interim the Loire had iced over, preventing his departure. Not until the last week in January 1777 would he be able sail on the first of two cruises in European waters.

First Cruise in British Waters

By 24 January 1777 the ice in the Loire River had thawed sufficiently to permit *Reprisal* to fall down to its mouth and stand out for the open sea on what would be a short but profitable cruise. From the closing days of January until mid-February, the ship cruised in the Bay of Biscay, capturing British merchantmen, and off the mouth of the English Channel looking for British packet boats from Falmouth. On 5 February *Reprisal* encountered H.M. packet *Swallow* (16 guns), Captain Charles Newman. Wickes realized this was the Lisbon packet he had orders to capture, in expectation that the ship would be transporting gold and silver. After *Reprisal* fired a number of ineffective broadsides into *Swallow,* Wickes grappled his prey. Sword in hand, he led the boarding party, and in a fierce engagement *Reprisal*'s crew suffered one sailor killed and several wounded. The American ship received a shot in the hull below the waterline causing a leak. Unfortunately, the packet was carrying neither cargo nor specie. Wickes, with his customary generosi-

continued on page 10

Life on Board a Continental Navy Warship

Life on board a warship during the American Revolution might seem harsh to the twenty-first-century sailor. Yet today's seaman would also find much that is familiar. The food was generally miserable, pay was small, discipline was strict, and work, especially at sea, was demanding. Even so, Congress made it clear that a ship's captain must look after the welfare of the men serving under his authority. The structure of ranks and ratings, organization of shipboard duties, and division of the crew into watches are aspects of shipboard life that have existed from the Navy's beginning.

The commanding officer of a naval vessel usually held the rank of captain in the Continental Navy and was commissioned by Congress. Nevertheless, even if he was a lieutenant, the crew addressed him as "captain," and he had the same authority and responsibility. An officer in command of a squadron would be addressed as "commodore." Each ship had one or more lieutenants, with the senior being the "first lieutenant" who was responsible to the captain for running the ship, much like an executive officer today. As there were no educational facilities on shore, young midshipmen learned how to be officers while serving on board ship.

Officers of another class held their rank by warrant rather than commission from Congress, and were more specialized in their duties. The sailing master was responsible, under the captain, for the safe conduct of the ship while underway. The ship's surgeon (when there was one) looked after the

Above, typical sailors of the era of the American Revolution. Right above, Topmen doing the dangerous job of furling a sail in a storm. Right, typical portside rigging.

health of the crew and treated those wounded in battle. The boatswain saw that all the items for working a ship (sails, rigging, boats, anchors) were accounted for and in good repair. The purser was in charge of the ship's stores and provisions, and kept track of the crew's pay. The master-at-arms maintained discipline. The gunner took charge of the ship's guns and all the implements needed to work them. The ship's carpenter and sailmaker were much like the damage control officers in the modern navy. They were in charge of repairing damage to the vessel and keeping the captain informed of the condition of the hull, masts, yards, deck, and sails.

The remaining crewmen were divided into three groups, depending on their experience and level of skill: petty officers, seamen, and landsmen. Petty officers were specialists like master's mates, boatswain's mates, quartermasters, and gunner's mates, who usually worked under a warrant officer, and were essential for the functioning and efficiency of the ship. When maneuvering in combat or in a storm, the ship's captain relied heavily on those rated as seamen: the crewmen that demonstrated the appropriate level of skill to handle the sails and rigging swiftly. The rest of the crew were rated as landsmen and were responsible for keeping the lower decks clean and manning the ship's guns in combat.

When underway, the captain divided the ship's company into two watches, "starboard" and "larboard" (port today), a system that divided the workload and ensured the manning of essential positions at all times. The day was divided into four-hour periods with the watches alternating the time that they were on duty. The 4 PM to 8 PM watch was usually divided in half—the first and the second "dog watches"—so that each watch would change duty hours the next day.

The workday began at 4 AM with the boatswain rousing the new watch with his boatswain's pipe. The men wetted down the deck, sprinkled sand, and scrubbed the planks with blocks of stones, a daily cleaning task known as holystoning. The crewmen swabbed the sand from the deck, and at 7:30 AM the previous watch was called to put up the hammocks. All hands were piped to breakfast at 8 AM after which the new watch holystoned the lower decks. The cook and his helpers served dinner at noon and supper at 4 PM. The rum ration was served at 12:30 PM. After supper the captain called the entire crew to battle stations and they prepared the

ship for action and inspection. At 8 PM the officers set the first night watch and the ship settled down for the night. During the day officers often drilled the crew at the guns or in the use of muskets and hand-to-hand weapons. Sometimes off-duty crewmen were allowed to mend clothes, learn seamanship skills, or crawl up in a corner and catch up on sleep.

Congress set the amount of pay and food each man on board ship received. Pay ranged from $6.66 per month for an able seaman to $32 per month for the captain. Warrant officers received fifteen dollars per month and petty officers received about ten dollars per month. Food rations included one pound of bread and one pound of beef or pork each day. Peas, rice, butter, cheese, turnips, potatoes, and onions were not issued every day, but they supplemented the diet. Congress encouraged commanding officers to add fresh items from local sources as opportunity offered. Finally, each man was allowed half a pint of rum per day.

Congress authorized the captain of a Continental Navy vessel to discipline and punish the crew for minor offenses such as cursing and drunkenness. Congress encouraged the captain to be vigilant and creative in this regard. An offender might be fined, put in irons, made to wear some badge of shame (like a wooden collar), or receive up to twelve lashes with a cat-o'-nine-tails. If the captain decided that the offense merited more lashes, he would need to ask for a court-martial. Court-martial offenses included stealing, quarreling or fighting with shipmates, provoking speech, and sleeping on watch. Desertion and murder could be punished by death.

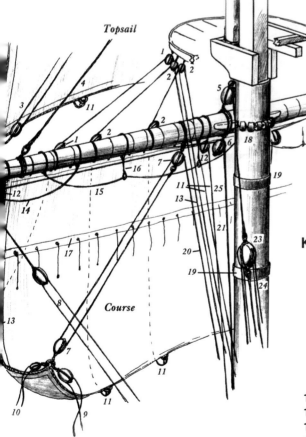

Key to rigging diagram

1. Leech line blocks
2. Buntline blocks
3. Clew
4. Lift
5. Lower halyard jeer block
6. Topsail sheet blocks
7. Clew garnet blocks
8. Brace
9. Sheet
10. Tack
11. Buntlines
12. Reef tackle blocks
13. Leech line

14. Flemish horse
15. Foot ropes
16. Stirrup
17. Reef band and reef
18. Parrels
19. Mast hoops
20. Clew garnet
21. Topsail sheet
22. Bowline
23. Lower halyard block
24. Lower halyard falls
25. Reef tackle falls

ty, returned the private adventures to *Swallow's* officers and passengers.

Having captured four merchantmen in addition to the Lisbon packet, *Reprisal* now had nearly eighty British prisoners on board. With prize crews sent on board the captured vessels to carry them into French ports, *Reprisal's* complement had fallen to a dangerous low of about eighty Americans. Fearing that the prisoners might rise and overwhelm the crew, Wickes decided to return to port. After a difficult passage of eight days, *Reprisal* arrived safely at Port Louis near Lorient, France, on 13 February. The cruise had been a complete success, with all five prizes reaching French ports.

The question immediately arose as to what to do with the British prisoners. Hearing that the British had captured two American privateers, Wickes wrote to the commissioners proposing that his prisoners be held in hopes that an exchange could be arranged with the British. These sentiments anticipated those of Captain John Paul Jones in 1778 after his cruise around the British Isles in *Ranger*. On 15 February Wickes sent on shore the five British captains and passengers on their parole and word of honor not to write to England, leave Port Louis, or otherwise cause trouble. Meanwhile, he went in his longboat to Port Louis to report to the registrar of the Admiralty the arrival of *Reprisal* and five other vessels, all his property, forced in by stress of weather.

On 18 February one of the *Swallow's* passengers, John Hunter, violated the terms of his parole by lodging a protest with the registrar of the Admiralty at Port Louis; and the next day another prisoner, Captain Charles Newman, as "an officer of His Britannic Majesty" appeared before the Intendant at Lorient, demanding freedom for his crew and the crews of the four other vessels. Later on 19 February Wickes met with the Intendant only to find that he wished to come on board to examine and discharge all seamen who chose to depart with Captain Newman. Wickes refused and countered that he would discharge all prisoners taken on his last cruise on being given a certificate for them from the Intendant.

Not hearing from the commissioners about his proposed prisoner exchange and after much negotiation with the British captains, Wickes eventually landed seventy-two British prisoners at Lorient and again with his accustomed generosity returned to each all of his clothes. Five of the prisoners agreed to sign on as crew of *Reprisal*.

The British government did not endure *Reprisal's* seizure of five British vessels quietly. When Wickes

returned on 14 February to Lorient with his prizes, Britain's ambassador to France, Viscount Stormont, lodged a vehement protest. The British demanded the restoration of the prizes and the expulsion of the *Reprisal*. Unfortunately for the British, Wickes disposed of the five prizes quickly and secretly before such restitution could be made. Vergennes disavowed French collusion in selling the prizes and sought to assure Stormont that the American warship would be directed to leave. On 20 February an Admiralty Court official told Wickes his vessels must depart within twenty-four hours. Wickes answered that the prizes would sail on the first favorable wind, but *Reprisal* was in need of repairs and must heave down, permission for which he had already asked. The commissioners, he said, were seeking the liberty of the port for *Reprisal*.

Between 22 and 25 February Thomas Morris, Continental Commercial Agent at Nantes, quietly disposed of all four of the merchantmen, bringing in a total of 90,000 livres. Wickes handled the *Swallow's* sale, because, according to a resolution of Congress, a vessel belonging to the British Crown became the property of the Continental Navy ship that captured it. Bérard Frères & Co. bought the *Swallow* for 16,000 livres and changed the name to *Marguerite*.

Undermining French Neutrality

By means of *Reprisal's* repeated and flagrant violations of French neutrality, Lambert Wickes sought to push France and Great Britain into war. Under the Treaty of Utrecht (1713), France and Great Britain were prohibited from opening their ports, either as bases for warships or as markets in which to sell prizes, to vessels of countries at war with the other. Cases of distress caused by weather or want of provisions constituted the one exception, and French authorities seized on this exception as a means of giving succor to Continental Navy ships and their prizes. Even a certain amount of clandestine prize sales could be winked at. However, the open and numerous violations increased the likelihood of an open breach with Britain. France's foreign minister, Comte de Vergennes, welcomed such a conflict, but not until France's armed forces were ready. Thus, while it sought to encourage the Americans in their quest for independence, France dared not tax Britain's patience too far.

Igniting a war between the House of Hanover and the House of Bourbon was exactly what the American commissioners to the Court of France and Lambert

"The hearts of the French are universally for us, and the Cry is strong for immediate War with Britain."

Wickes sought to do. In a frank statement of American motives at this time, William Carmichael, an intimate friend of two of the American commissioners, Silas Deane and Benjamin Franklin, wrote to William Bingham in Martinique: "It is our business to force on a war, in spite of . . . [French] inclinations to the contrary, for which purpose I see nothing so likely as fitting out privateers from the ports and Islands of France." A dispatch to Congress from the commissioners, although couched in more guarded language than Carmichael's, also hinted at American objectives: "The hearts of the French are universally for us, and the Cry is strong for immediate War with Britain. Indeed everything tends that way, but the Court has its reasons for postponing it a little longer." On 28 February Wickes wrote the Committee of Secret Correspondence: ". . . those orders [to depart] from the French Ministry I look on as Fenness [finesse: adroit maneuvering; trick or stratagem] and only given to Save appearances and gain time, as they are not yet quite ready for a Warr, but I think it will certainly take place in May or June." On 20 July, Wickes wrote enthusiastically to Captain Henry Johnson, "our late Cruize has made a great deal of Noise & will Probably Soon bring on a Warr between France and England which is my Sincere Wish." The commissioners hoped that the captures made by Reprisal and other Continental Navy ships that they might send out would bring the mind of the French Court into accord with the hearts of the French people sooner rather than later.

Plans for Naval Operations in British Waters

On 25 February the American commissioners wrote Wickes soliciting his opinion on three proposed plans for naval operations in the spring and summer of 1777. Wickes believed a cruise in the North Sea targeting the British Baltic trade too dangerous, as he did not know the waters and did not have the necessary charts. Although he believed a cruise on the Guinea coast to be a better option, he found it utterly impracticable for Reprisal, as the cruise would require two months' more fresh water and provisions than the ship could carry. Wickes also thought that a cruise off the

French coast would prove unsuccessful, as three or more British ships of the line patrolled the Bay of Biscay. He strongly favored purchasing a fast cutter to be stationed at Dunkirk, where it could run into the Downs, a roadstead and anchorage in the English Channel off Deal, England, and cut out British ships with impunity, but this could only happen if the cutter and prizes received protection at Dunkirk. As soon as he saw Reprisal hove down at Lorient to have its bottom examined and cleaned, Wickes set out for Paris on 16 March to consult with the commissioners.

On his arrival in Paris on 22 March, Wickes learned that the commissioners had purchased a second vessel, a Dover (Folkestone) cutter, in England, which they were having fitted out to sail in company with Reprisal. The commissioners gave command of the Continental Navy cutter Dolphin to Samuel Nicholson, to whom Silas Deane delivered a commission as a captain in the navy on 7 April, backdated to 10 December 1776.

By early April Wickes and the commissioners had formulated a broad plan of naval operations in European waters for the spring and summer of 1777. First, the Continental Navy lugger Surprize, commanded by Captain Gustavus Conyngham, would conduct raids out of Dunkirk. Second, the cutter Dolphin at Le Havre would be brought to Nantes by its French crew and turned over to Captain Samuel Nicholson, who would supervise its arming and fitting out as a Continental Navy vessel. Third, Reprisal and Dolphin would sail through the Irish Sea entering through St. Georges Channel to intercept the Irish linen fleet and disrupt the trade from Dublin. And fourth, Captain Thomas Bell would endeavor to purchase and arm a vessel at Genoa, Italy, and operate out of Marseilles in the Mediterranean. The last part of the plan never came to fruition.

Dolphin arrived on 10 April at Pellerin, a small town just below Nantes, and the refit commenced immediately, overseen by Nicholson and Wickes. They armed the cutter with ten 3-pounder carriage guns and fourteen swivels. As usual, manning proved to be the biggest problem. The crew eventually numbered thirty-five seamen, of whom fifteen were Frenchmen. The Dolphin was not ready for sea until 15 May. Meanwhile, the Continental Navy brigantine

Lexington, Captain Henry Johnson, arrived at Bordeaux, and Wickes wrote the commissioners suggesting that *Lexington* cruise with *Reprisal* and *Dolphin*. The commissioners concurred and ordered Johnson to join Wickes.

On Wickes' return to Lorient on 25 April, he found the crew of *Reprisal* grumbling over the non-payment of prize money, something he had anticipated on reading his initial orders from the Committee of Secret Correspondence. No prize money meant trouble. The next day the crew refused to go to sea until they received their prize money. Most had enlisted in *Reprisal* for one year and their time was up. Wickes, sympathizing with his men, explained to them that his instructions prevented him from paying out prize shares until *Reprisal* returned to Philadelphia. He prevailed on his crew to sail to Nantes, where he promised that he would procure part of their prize money from Thomas Morris, the Continental Commercial Agent. On 27 April Wickes appealed to the commissioners to give Thomas Morris prompt orders to prevent delays in the payment. Somehow Wickes persuaded Morris to give him enough money to make a partial payment of five gold louis to each officer, warrant officer, petty officer, and seaman, thereby quelling the mutiny. Wickes' swift and adroit actions defused an otherwise explosive situation.

The disposal of prizes posed a continuing problem. The French might feign surprise and find an excuse to explain to the British how three Continental Navy ships were allowed to sail from their ports to attack British coastal shipping, but they could never justify letting them reenter with prizes. To circumvent this difficulty, Wickes resorted to the same measures adopted during his first cruise. He ordered Johnson and Nicholson that whenever they took a prize the entire crew was to be taken out and replaced by some of their own seamen. False papers would then be drawn up so that the vessel, documented as an American merchantman from a port determined by the cargo it had on board, could be sent into a French port. This subterfuge would allow the Americans time to dispose of their prizes in hastily arranged sales.

Second Cruise in British Waters

Wickes' squadron sailed on 28 May on what would be a precedent-setting cruise. It was the first appearance of a Continental Navy squadron in European

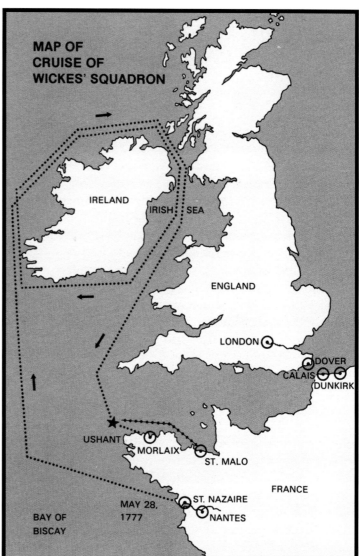

Cruise of Wickes' Squadron in British waters.

waters and the first forward deployment of an American naval squadron in foreign waters. Two days out, a British ship of the line chased the squadron, but the Americans escaped. Contrary winds prevented them from entering the Irish Sea from the south, so they sailed clockwise around the west coast of Ireland, taking no prizes until they entered the North Channel to the Irish Sea and approached the shipping lanes out of Glasgow and Greenock. On 18 June they took their first prizes off the Mull of Kintyre, Scotland—two brigs and two sloops. The squadron remained off the Mull of Kintyre for three more days, capturing five additional prizes. During the week following, Wickes' squadron cruised in the Irish Sea just off the east coast of Ireland, making nine additional captures. Of the eighteen vessels captured, Wickes sent eight into French ports, released three, and sank seven.

This bold strike at British shipping right on England's doorstep caused insurance rates to climb and prompted angry demands for increased naval protection from that country's mercantile community. In fact, the alarm caused by Wickes' activities delayed the sailing of the Irish linen fleet until the Royal Navy could provide protection. Jonathan Williams, Jr., Continental Commercial Agent at Nantes, informed Congress that Wickes' squadron had "created an universal Terror in all the Seaports throughout Ireland and on that side of England and Scotland," adding that "in some places they muster'd their militia in apprehension of a Descent, and their fears have taught them to respect our naval Force."

While returning to France at the end of their month's cruise, Wickes' squadron fell in with a large ship they believed to be a richly laden West Indiaman homeward-bound. Actually, the vessel was the 74-gun ship of the line HMS *Burford*, which gave chase. As the large ship gained on the squadron, Wickes gave the signal for the ships to separate, knowing full well that the enemy would pursue *Reprisal*, which was the largest potential prize. In a remarkable display of loyalty to his captain and his ship, instead of doubling off, Henry Lawrence, prize master of the snow *Friendship* in company with the squadron, threw his vessel in the path of the on-coming *Burford*, risking an English prison in order to divert it from the Continental Navy ships. *Burford* ignored the bait and bore down on *Reprisal*. During a chase lasting twelve hours in which *Burford* approached almost within musket range of *Reprisal*, Wickes found the necessary speed to escape only by throwing overboard all his ship's 6-pounders and sawing through four beams to lighten ship and increase resiliency. According to Wickes' principal biographer, William Bell Clark, "only a master of seamanship and strategy, backed by determination that never admitted defeat, could have carried her safely through."

Detained in France

When *Reprisal* reached haven in the port of St. Malo on the north coast of Brittany on 27 June, the city's inhabitants greeted it with cheers and unbridled joy. Despite having barely eluded capture, Wickes considered his second cruise a complete success. His report to the commissioners reflects his modesty and willingness to give credit to others. He praised Henry Johnson thus: "As I had not the pleasure of knowing Captain Johnson before I could not give him a Caracter Sufficient to his Merrit & Now beg leave to recommend him as a Very brave Active Officer & worthy your Honours utmost Attention."

Wickes wrote the commissioners on 4 July, the first anniversary of the Declaration of Independence, "I think there is little Prospect of doing any thing more on this Coast & am in hopes you will order Capt Johnson and me to Proceed for America together." He began *Reprisal's* refit for the return voyage to Philadelphia. Within two weeks, however, King Louis XVI ordered the American warships detained, the French members of their crews placed under arrest, and Wickes and his fellow captains compelled to sign paroles that they would not leave France without the Minister of Marine's permission.

By using French ports as bases for his cruises in British waters, Wickes had brought France and Great Britain to the brink of war, as he had hoped to do. France sought to pull itself back from that brink, but to do so without harming the American cause. Thanks in part to Wickes' manipulations, the British, outraged by what they saw as French collusion in American depredations on British commerce, demanded that the French expel the American warships from French ports, leaving those ships to their chances of being captured by the British navy. In response, the French government tried to mollify the British by assuring them that the Americans would be confined to port and not be allowed to cruise. The British refused to accept this resolution of the dispute and strongly hinted that the French could either sacrifice the American cruisers or have war. Because its navy was not yet mobilized, the French chose to sacrifice the Americans. They finally ordered the Continental Navy vessels to sail and not to return to French ports.

The End of a Glorious Career

The commissioners on 9 September ordered Wickes in *Reprisal* and Johnson in *Lexington* to return in company to Portsmouth, N.H., or Boston, with dispatches for the Continental Congress. The commissioners intended to convert *Dolphin*, the third vessel in Wickes' squadron, into a packet for their use. *Reprisal* got underway from St. Malo on 14 September, and *Lexington* sailed on 17 September from Morlaix. H.M. cutter *Alert* captured *Lexington* on 19 September in the English Channel. *Reprisal's* fate was even grimmer.

Mysteries of ships that sailed over the horizon never to be seen again litter the annals of the world's navies. *Reprisal's* case is different. Because of one fortunate sailor, we know where and how *Reprisal* and its gallant captain and crew perished. Three days' sail past the

Engagement between Continental Navy brigantine Lexington *and HM cutter* Alert.

Newfoundland Banks a gale struck the ship, and "the ship was pooped with three heavy seas, which carried her down." A pair of men saved themselves by clinging to a gangway ladder. Two days after the sinking, one of the two survivors gave out through exhaustion and sank beneath the waves. The same day, a French vessel destined for Bordeaux, France, plucked from the sea the sole remaining survivor, Nathan Jaquays, *Reprisal*'s cook.

How then do we assess Lambert Wickes and his naval service; what is his significance; and why should he be remembered? Reporting to the Continental Congress the news of Wickes' death, Benjamin Franklin wrote, "This Loss is extreamly to be lamented; as he was a gallant Officer and a very worthy Man." In concurrence with Franklin, we should remember Wickes for his outstanding qualities as a leader. He was intrepid, brave, deferential to civilian authority, considerate of the sailors under him, and a thoroughly accomplished mariner. In short, he possessed all the attributes of a fine naval officer. Among naval historians, Wickes' standing is very high. Samuel Eliot Morison ranks him among the top four captains of the Continental Navy, the other three being John Paul Jones, John Barry, and Nicholas Biddle. James Fenimore Cooper, himself an officer in the early sailing navy, lauded Wickes for his efforts in carrying the war to British waters, writing that the Marylander always performed his duty "with discretion, spirit, and steadiness." Wickes' biographer, William Bell Clark, admired his fortitude, forbearance, and tenacity of purpose. But in his estimation the most outstanding characteristic of Lambert Wickes was his innate modesty. No other captain so shrank from using superlatives when describing his own accomplishments as did Wickes. And it was because of this aversion to self-promotion, Clark argues, that Wickes is so little known today.

Lambert Wickes, captain, Continental Navy, commanded the first warship of the United States in Europe, led America's first forward-deployed squadron in enemy waters, set the precedent of bringing the war close to the British homeland followed by Continental Navy captains Gustavus Conyngham and John Paul Jones, and promoted the diplomatic goal of bringing France into the war. For these accomplishments he deserves to be remembered, but it is his leadership qualities of initiative, obedience to orders, care for his men, seamanship, and modesty that deserve emulation.

The American Commissioners to France

On 24 September 1776 the Continental Congress voted to send three commissioners to France to represent the newly independent United States and appointed Benjamin Franklin, Silas Deane, and Arthur Lee to the posts. Franklin (1706–1790) was possibly the best-known American at that time. A former printer and colonial agent, he had a worldwide reputation as a writer and scientist. Though fiercely patriotic, Franklin also came across as cosmopolitan, tolerant, and open to intellectual developments. Arthur Lee (1740–1792), though young, had already dabbled in a variety of occupations—physician, lawyer, political essayist, colonial agent, and even intelligence operative—before deciding to become a diplomat. Upright, intelligent, and fiercely patriotic, but also arrogant, suspicious to the point of paranoia, and over-zealous, Lee could be a difficult colleague and during his time in Europe hurt the American cause as often as he aided it. At the time of his appointment, Lee resided in England where he had served as agent for the colony of Massachusetts. The third commissioner was Silas Deane (1737–1789), a former Connecticut politician. One historian has described him as "pompous, convivial, somewhat less than honest (although careful to hide it), braggingly patriotic, and rather unintelligent." At the time of his appointment, Deane served in France as a purchasing agent for Congress. In 1778 Congress recalled Deane and sent John Adams (1735–1826), a Massachusetts lawyer, scholar, and politician, to take his place.

The commissioners' primary task was to persuade the government of France to expand its support of the American revolutionaries and to offer the French a treaty of friendship and commerce. In the month following their appointment, Congress gave the commissioners authority to negotiate commercial treaties with other European nations

Silas Deane, the American Commissioner to France who most directly oversaw naval affairs.

and to obtain the loan or sale of eight French ships of the line. In October, the congressional Committee of Secret Correspondence added another significant task to the commissioners' docket. The committee had instructed Lambert Wickes, who was transporting Franklin to France, to land Franklin and then cruise the English Channel, attacking and capturing British merchant ships. Assuming success in that endeavor, the committee directed Wickes to send these prizes into French ports and instructed the commissioners to try to persuade the French government to allow Wickes and other American captains to use its ports to dispose of captured prizes, to escape British pursuers, and to refit their ships if necessary. The request was to be made despite the fact that the French had a treaty of neutrality with the English. In other words, American naval vessels were to act in a provocative manner to promote tension, and maybe even war, between the French and British, and the commissioners were to aid and abet this effort.

As seen in the chapters on Wickes and Gustavus Conyngham, the Americans used French ports and succeeded in creating tension between the French and the English. That tension contributed to the French decision to enter an alliance with the United States. With the signing of the treaty on 6 February 1778, the American commissioners completed their primary mission.

The French acknowledged the new alliance by sending a minister to America. Because diplomatic etiquette demanded that the United States have someone of equal rank representing them at the French Court, the American commissioners were replaced by a minister plenipotentiary. Franklin was named minister. Of the other commissioners, Adams became minister to the Netherlands and Lee was recalled home.

Gustavus Conyngham

By Mark L. Hayes

During the year before France actively entered the war in the spring of 1778, the Americans intensified their efforts to attack British trade at sea. Most American vessels operating in European waters originally came from the United States, and the majority of these were privateers commissioned by state governments. They had a significant effect on British trade, as the many captures forced merchants to pay high insurance rates or send their cargo in foreign ships. The most successful of the American captains during this phase of the war was not a privateer but a captain in the Continental Navy, Gustavus Conyngham. Between May 1777 and May 1778, he captured twenty-four ships and became one of the most hated men in England, his name and his exploits filling London newspapers and diplomatic letters.

Apprenticeship to Command

Like so many Americans who fought during the War for Independence, Gustavus Conyngham began his life overseas. Born in the Irish county of Donegal in 1747, he immigrated to Philadelphia, Pennsylvania, in 1763 with his mother and father. The Conynghams were from a distinguished, land owning family, and Gustavus's cousin Redmond founded, with John Nesbitt, a Philadelphia shipping company. Forgoing further schooling, the young Conyngham entered his cousin's service and became an apprentice to a Captain Henderson, who regularly carried goods to and from Antigua, a British island in the Caribbean Sea.

Gustavus became fascinated with the ocean, and with teenage enthusiasm sought to learn all he could from the experienced seamen around him. Impressed with the boy's eagerness and with no children of his own, Captain Henderson set out to train and teach him about sailing a ship and the business of the Antiguan trade. It was demanding work, but young Conyngham rose to the challenge and matured as he took on greater responsibilities. He gained leadership as well as seamanship skills under Henderson's fatherly guidance.

Above, Captain Gustavus Conyngham. Right, Philadelphia waterfront where Conyngham spent much of his adult life.

Redmond Conyngham's son David took his father's place at the head of the shipping house when the latter returned to Ireland. After Captain Henderson died, David promoted his cousin to command the vessel in which he had served for several years. In 1773, at the age of twenty-six, Gustavus married Anne Hockley, the American-born daughter of a Philadelphia merchant, and they soon added children to their new family. By 1775 the Conynghams enjoyed a comfortable and successful life that would soon be altered by monumental events.

The first shots of the American War for Independence were fired in Massachusetts in April 1775, and thousands of men converged on Boston, determined to defend their freedom. This American army required huge quantities of basic supplies to maintain it in the field, and many of those supplies would need to come from overseas. The merchant company of Conyngham and Nesbitt decided to take a financial risk by sending its vessels through waters dominated by the Royal Navy in order to bring back the necessary war supplies.

Charming Peggy was one of these merchant vessels, sent from Philadelphia to Holland to obtain saltpeter, clothing, muskets, and other munitions for General George Washington's men. It would be a dangerous and important mission, and David Conyngham, along with John Nesbitt, offered command to the young but experienced Gustavus. *Charming Peggy* set sail in the fall of 1775 and after a twenty-three day voyage across the Atlantic entered the English Channel. Despite Captain Conyngham's attempt to take advantage of the channel fog, a British frigate soon spotted his vessel and ordered him to heave to. Convinced that he

Small British frigates such as the one pictured here were constantly on the lookout for American merchant vessels.

had stopped a Yankee smuggler, the British captain placed a prize crew on board *Charming Peggy* with orders to carry it into the English port of Plymouth.

Unwilling to accept his fate, Conyngham waited for the right moment and quickly regained control of his ship. This time he successfully used the fog to slip away from the frigate and brought *Charming Peggy* in behind Texel Island in Holland. The Conynghams' attempt to bring back military supplies to America came to naught as British representatives complained to Dutch authorities, who prevented the vessel's sailing. Gustavus debated whether or not to sneak out of port, but, as his ship was a dull sailer, he considered his chances to escape to be too low. Distraught and out of options, the Americans decided to sell *Charming Peggy* and separately seek their way home.

Continental Navy Commission and Cruise of *Surprize*

Gustavus hoped to command a vessel carrying supplies back to America, but he could not find even one to carry him back to Philadelphia. For over a year he languished in French ports until he heard of the arrival of the American commissioners in France. One of the commissioners, the famous Benjamin Franklin, carried several blank commissions signed by the Continental Congress, and instructions to purchase and man ships in Europe to cruise against British trade. Conyngham arranged a meeting with Franklin, who was impressed with the thirty-year old captain. Gustavus received one of Franklin's commissions on 1 March 1777 and became a captain in the Continental Navy.

Sailing vessels of the day

(not to scale)

1.

5.

1. Brig
2. Brigantine
3. Cutter
4. Frigate
5. Galley
6. Ketch
7. Douarnenez Lugger
8. Schooner
9. Sloop
10. Ship-of-the-Line 1795

2.

6.

3.

7.

8.

4.

9.

10.

In CONGRESS.

The DELEGATES of the UNITED COLONIES of New-Hampshire, Massachusetts Bay, Rhode-Island, Connecticut, New-York, New-Jersey, Pennsylvania, the Counties of New-Castle, Kent, and Sussex on Delaware, Maryland, Virginia, North-Carolina, South-Carolina, and Georgia, to *Gustavus Cunningham*

WE reposing especial Trust and Confidence in your Patriotism, Valour, Conduct and Fidelity, DO by these Presents, constitute and appoint you to be *Commander* of the Armed *Vessel* called the *Surprise* in the service of the Thirteen United Colonies of North-America, fitted out for the defence of American Liberty, and for repelling every hostile Invasion thereof. You are therefore carefully and diligently to discharge the Duty of *Commander on board said Vessel* by doing and performing all Manner of Things thereunto belonging. And we do strictly charge and require all Officers, Marines and Seamen under your Command, to be obedient to your Orders as *directed by Congress* And you are to observe and follow such Orders and Directions from Time to Time, as you shall receive from this or a future Congress of the United Colonies, or Committee of Congress, for that Purpose appointed, or Commander in Chief for the Time being of the Navy of the United Colonies, or any other your superior Officer, according to the Rules and Discipline of War, the Usage of the Sea, and the Instructions herewith given you, in Pursuance of the Trust reposed in you. This Commission to continue in Force untill revoked by this or a future Congress.

Baltimore
March 1.st 1777

By Order of the Congress
John Hancock PRESIDENT.

Attest. *Cha Thomson Secy*

The commission issued to Conyngham by Benjamin Franklin, signed by John Hancock, making him a commanding officer in the Continental Navy. (Courtesy, Collection of the New-York Historical Society, negative number 49453.)

With the assistance of American merchants John Ross and William Hodge, the commissioners searched for a suitable vessel for Conyngham to command. One was found in England: a small vessel named *Peacock*. The soon-to-be Continental Navy lugger *Surprize* was purchased under false names with John Beach, who claimed to be an Irishman, assigned as her master. Although born in Dublin, Beach made his home in Philadelphia, and he was handpicked by Conyngham to be his first lieutenant. The vessel was brought to Dunkirk on the northwest coast of France where William Hodge had it fitted out for its first cruise. On 1 May 1777, Beach took the unarmed lugger out to sea with papers stating that it was bound for Norderoerne in the Faeroes Islands. However, *Surprize* moored just outside the harbor, and that night Conyngham quietly came on board with carriage and swivel guns, as well as extra crewmen, transforming the vessel into a warship. Gustavus was pleased with his mostly American and deeply patriotic crew. The new Continental Navy captain took *Surprize*, armed and ready, into the English Channel and began his assault on British shipping.

The next day, toward evening, the crew spotted the English packet sloop *Prince of Orange* carrying mail between Harwich and the Dutch port of Hellevoetsluys. Conyngham brought *Surprize* alongside the British vessel and engaged its captain, William Story, in casual conversation while studying the packet's ability to defend itself. Satisfied, Gustavus ordered his crew to bring the lugger close aboard his prey and to run up the American ensign of thirteen red and white stripes. Intending to board the packet, Conyngham called for Story to surrender his vessel to the Congress of the United States. The British captain complied, and an eleven-man prize crew led by Lieutenant John Beach climbed over the bulwarks and took control. The captors transferred ten crewmen of the packet to *Surprize*, where they were handcuffed for

Manning the Continental Navy

Finding men to serve in the vessels of the Continental Navy was an on-going struggle. Privateers, privately owned ships whose captains were given governmental authority to capture enemy ships, competed against the Navy for the services of the small pool of qualified potential American seamen. Americans operated more than two thousand private armed vessels during the American Revolution. Not only were privateers numerous, they were also a more lucrative berth for most seamen. Privateers paid higher wages than the Navy—$16 per month versus $6.66 per month for the Navy—and they rewarded their crews with a higher percentage of the value of any enemy ship they captured. As a result, Continental Navy captains had a hard time finding and keeping crews and resorted to novel solutions to keep their vessels at sea.

In his cruise in the Caribbean in 1776, for example, Lambert Wickes filled out his crew using thirty-nine captured British seamen after sending forty-three of his original crew of eighty-seven to sail three captured vessels to American ports. In order to man the *Revenge* when it left Dunkirk, France, in July 1777, Gustavus Conyngham employed non-Americans, mostly French seamen. Since a majority of the crew was French, one wonders if French or English was the language used for transmitting orders on board this American warship. The most extreme example of a hybrid crew may have been *Bonhomme Richard*'s in June 1779, when John Paul Jones sailed from Lorient, France. Jones' crew at that time consisted of 79 Americans, including the overwhelming majority of the officers; 174 Frenchmen, including 137 French marines and 36 French "landsmen" (mostly peas-

GREAT
ENCOURAGEMENT
FOR
SEAMEN.

ALL GENTLEMEN SEAMEN and able-bodied LANDSMEN who have a Mind to diftinguish themfelves in the GLORIOUS CAUSE of their Country, and make their Fortunes, an Opportunity now offers on board the Ship RANGER, of Twenty Guns, (for France) now laying in Portsmouth, in the State of New-Hampshire, commanded by JOHN PAUL JONES Efq; let them repair to the Ship's Rendezvous in Portsmouth, or at the Sign of Commodore Manley, in Salem, where they will be kindly entertained, and receive the greateft Encouragement.---The Ship Ranger, in the Opinion of every Perfon who has feen her is looked upon to be one of the beft Cruizers in America.----She will be always able to Fight her Guns under a moft excellent Cover ; and no Veffel yet built was ever calculated for failing fafter, and making good Weather.

Any Gentlemen Volunteers who have a Mind to take an agreable Voyage in this pleafant Seafon of the Year, may, by entering on board the above Ship Ranger, meet with every Civility they can poffibly expect, and for a further Encouragement depend on the firft Opportunity being embraced to reward each one agreable to his Merit.

All reafonable Travelling Expences will be allowed, and the Advance-Money be paid on their Appearance on Board.

In CONGRESS, March 29, 1777.

RESOLVED,

THAT the Marine Committee be authorifed to advance to every able Seaman, that enters into the Continental Service, any Sum not exceeding FORTY DOLLARS, and to every ordinary Seaman or Landfman, any Sum not exceeding TWENTY DOLLARS, to be deducted from their future Prize-Money.

By Order of Congress,
JOHN HANCOCK, President.

DANVERS: Printed by E. Russell, at the Houfe late the Bell-Tavern.

A 1777 recruiting poster for John Paul Jones' Ranger.

ants and fishermen from Brittany); 59 English sailors, most of whom were prisoners of war taken from French prisons; 29 Portuguese; 21 Irishmen; 4 Scotsmen; 7 Norwegians; 2 East Indians; 1 Swiss; and 1 Italian sailor. That these captains and their officers could mold such motley material into crews that functioned well in the heat of battle speaks of their talent as leaders and commanders.

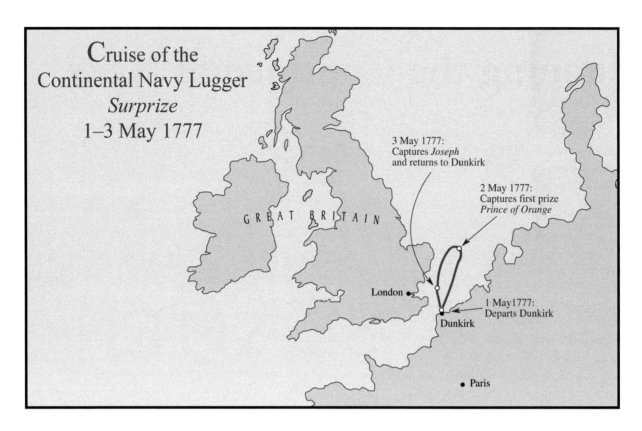

Cruise of the
Continental Navy Lugger
Surprize
1–3 May 1777

3 May 1777:
Captures *Joseph*
and returns to Dunkirk

2 May 1777:
Captures first prize
Prince of Orange

GREAT BRITAIN

London

1 May 1777:
Departs Dunkirk

Dunkirk

Paris

the night. Story, the steward, and the passengers remained on board *Prince of Orange* under a strong guard. One of the passengers, His Majesty's Messenger Mr. Lawson, had the presence of mind to fake an illness so that he would be left alone, and he threw all the dispatches out his cabin window undetected.

The following morning prize and captor met a Dutch fishing vessel, which Conyngham hired to carry the captain, crew, and passengers into Holland. Emphasizing the point that he was no pirate, Gustavus returned the clothing, money, personal articles, and jewelry to his prisoners before turning them loose, then fired a three-gun salute as they parted company. This gallant conduct, reported in English newspapers, would serve him well when a British privateer captured him two years later.

It was widely understood by Americans in Europe that the ports of France and Spain would be open to their privateers and merchant vessels, as well as the sale of prizes. With this in mind,

Een Engelsche Paket-boot door een Americaansche Kaaper genoomen, den 2 May A.º 1777.

Above, Conyngham, in the Continental Navy lugger Surprize, *captures the royal packet* Prince of Orange *on 3 May 1777. Left, Dunkirk, France, where Conyngham acquired both of his vessels.*

Conyngham ordered *Surprize* and *Prince of Orange* back to Dunkirk. The next day the Americans intercepted a ship flying the British flag. Gustavus hailed it and discovered that it was the brigantine *Joseph*, under the command of Captain Robert Kelly, sailing for Hamburg in Germany with a cargo of fruit and wine. Kelly obeyed the American's call to surrender, and a prize crew of eight men took control of the British vessel. Again meeting a fishing boat, Conyngham transferred *Joseph*'s crew and sent them ashore. About three o'clock that afternoon, *Surprize* and her two prizes entered the port at Dunkirk.

As the Americans neared the shore, two English ketches, their captains bent on mischief, deliberately and repeatedly collided with

Conyngham's vessels. *Surprize* and *Prince of Orange* suffered severe damage from the violent jolting, which started several leaks. Conyngham and Beach filed protests against the masters of the ketches, hoping to recover the cost of repairs and loss of cargo, but the Americans soon faced much more serious problems.

The city of Dunkirk was unique among French ports. Having fitted out many privateers to cruise against British shipping during the Nine Years War (1689–1697) and the War of the Spanish Succession (1702–1713), the French promised not to fit out any more at Dunkirk and accepted official British observers at the port as part of the Treaty of Utrecht (1713). As a result, it was the one port in France in which the French could not possibly get away with accepting American privateers and prizes. Conyngham

continued on page 28

Revolutionary War Captains Remembered

Above, Wickes, *Destroyer No. 75.* Below, Wickes, *DD 578.*

While most Americans recognize the name John Paul Jones, fewer recognize the names of Lambert Wickes and Gustavus Conyngham. The United States Navy, however, has memorialized all three of these founders of the American naval tradition by christening warships after them.

Two United States destroyers have borne Lambert Wickes' name. *Wickes* (Destroyer No. 75), built in 1918, served as a convoy escort during World War I and in 1940 was turned over to the Royal Navy as part of the Lend Lease Agreement, serving as HMS *Montgomery* from October 1940 until February 1944. The second *Wickes* (DD 578), built in 1942–1943 as one of the famous *Fletcher*-class destroyers, took part in most of the Leyte Gulf operations of October–November 1944, the liberation of the Philippines, and in the Okinawa campaign, earning five battle stars for its World War II service.

The Navy commissioned the original *Conyngham* (DD 58) on 21 January 1916. The ship was among the first American destroyers that joined British

forces for convoy duty after the United States entered World War I in April 1917. The second *Conyngham* (DD 371) entered the Navy on 4 November 1936. During World War II, the destroyer shot down several Japanese planes at Pearl Harbor and protected aircraft carriers at the battles of Midway and Santa Cruz in 1942. Assigned to General Douglas MacArthur's forces in the southwest Pacific in November 1942, *Conyngham* supported amphibious operations before returning to the Navy in the

Above, Conyngham, *DD 371. Below*, Conyngham, *DDG 17. Bottom*, Conyngham, *DD 58.*

Central Pacific just in time to support the assault in the Marianas in May 1944. It received fourteen battle stars for service in World War II. The third *Conyngham* (DDG 17) served in the U.S. Navy from 13 July 1963 through 30 October 1990. During its career, the guided missile destroyer made fifteen deployments to the Mediterranean Sea, including freedom of navigation cruises in the Black Sea and off Libya in the Gulf of Sidra, and provided gunfire support for the U.S. Marines at Beirut, Lebanon, in 1983. In 1987, *Conyngham* received the Navy Unit Commendation for its quick aid to the frigate *Stark* (FFG 31), crippled in the Persian Gulf by two hits from Iraqi antiship missiles.

Top, John Paul Jones, *DD 932 and DDG 32. Above,* Paul Jones, *DD 230. Below,* Paul Jones, *DD 10. Left,* Paul Jones, *Civil War side wheel steam gunboat.*

Five ships that served in the U.S. Navy honored John Paul Jones by carrying his name. The first three were simply named *Paul Jones.* The first of these was a sidewheel, double-ended, steam gunboat that served during the American Civil War. The second *Paul Jones* (DD 10) entered the Navy on 19 July 1902, and was stationed at San Francisco until World War I. Throughout the war, it remained in the western Atlantic, where on 2 July 1918 it rescued 1,250 U.S. Marines and officers from a burning transport off the coast of Virginia. The Navy commissioned the third *Paul Jones* (DD 230) on 19 April 1921. It served in the Asiatic Fleet in the western Pacific prior to the outbreak of WWII. After the Japanese attack on Pearl Harbor on 7 December 1941, *Paul Jones* joined Dutch naval units off Java, where it fought in two surface actions including the Battle of Java Sea on 27 February 1942. The American destroyer escaped destruction at the hands

of the Japanese fleet and spent the rest of the war on convoy duty in the eastern Pacific and Atlantic.

John Paul Jones (DD 932) entered service on 5 April 1956 and was the second of the initial class of destroyers of postwar design. It spent its career in the Atlantic and Mediterranean and took part in the quarantine of Cuba during the October 1962 crisis over the Soviet Union's deployment of ballistic missiles to the communist-controlled island. At the end of 1965 the destroyer sailed to Philadelphia where it underwent conversion to a guided missile destroyer. Reclassified DDG 32, it recommissioned in the fall of 1967 and deployed with the U.S. Seventh Fleet off the coast of Vietnam during the war. The guided missile destroyer continued to serve in the fleet until it was decommissioned on 15 December 1982.

John Paul Jones, *DDG 53*.

The latest ship to bear the name *John Paul Jones* (DDG 53) continues to serve in the U.S. Navy. Commissioned on 18 December 1993, it is the fourth ship of the powerful *Arleigh Burke* class of destroyers designed to engage land, air, surface, and subsurface targets simultaneously. *John Paul Jones* fired the first missiles in the War on Terrorism at targets in Afghanistan on 7 and 8 October 2001.

The American commissioners saw an opportunity to intercept British commerce in the unprotected northern approaches to Great Britain and launch raids on the west coast of England.

may have been ignorant of these facts, or his liberal and biased interpretation of prize law may have gotten the better of him. Benjamin Franklin labeled Conynham's act "imprudent," while a less kind French official called it "stupid."

Official British protests of the American actions quickly made their way to French officials. Not prepared for a major breach in Anglo-French relations, Louis XVI's minister for foreign affairs, the Comte de Vergennes, ordered the confiscation of Conyngham's prizes and jailed the American crew on 10 May. Three days later, the British ambassador, Lord Stormont, visited Vergennes, who greeted the ambassador with a smile, apparently pleased with his actions. The French minister emphasized that the king's desire for justice and equity motivated him to take the severe actions. Skeptical, the British government concluded that the French Court was willing to keep up the appearances of neutrality for the time being. A month later, the French released Conyngham and his crew from prison but returned his prizes to their British owners. Gustavus regretted that his men were denied prize money, and he hoped that Congress would provide them with some financial reward for their service.

Although he did not have anything to show for his efforts materially, Gustavus Conyngham's brief cruise strongly affected British seaborne commerce. Following the initial report of the capture of *Prince of Orange*, the British Admiralty ordered at least five warships to cruise the English Channel in search of *Surprize*. British insurance rates to cover shipping in the Channel immediately rose to 10 percent between Dover and Calais and temporarily to 40 percent for the Harwich to Hellevoetsluys packet. On the average, insurance rates in London increased to 28 percent from 1777 to 1778, higher than anytime during the global conflict of the Seven Years War (1756-1763).

The American commissioners saw an opportunity to intercept British commerce in the unprotected northern approaches to Great Britain and launch raids on the west coast of England. A squadron of three small Continental Navy vessels under Captain Lambert Wickes set sail from St. Nazaire, France, for those waters on 28 May. Franklin and Deane also sent a request to Congress asking that the Marine Committee send two or three frigates to cruise in British waters. In the meantime, the commissioners

worked to get Conyngham back out to sea and add to the pressure on enemy trade.

Getting Back to Sea

William Hodge searched the port of Dunkirk for a larger vessel to attack enemy shipping and settled on *Greyhound*, a large British cutter of about 130 tons. With the approval and help of Franklin and Deane, Hodge purchased the cutter and began to fit it out even while Conyngham and his crew were still in jail. After the French authorities released them on 10 June, Gustavus and his crew quickly joined Hodge in getting the vessel ready for sea. Hodge had acquired fourteen 4-pounder cannon to arm the cutter, and Conyngham found a place on shore to fire the guns, testing them for defects. Satisfied, the Americans placed them in the ship's hold rather than on deck in order to maintain the appearance of a merchant ship fitting out for a voyage across the Atlantic.

The British were not fooled by the American attempts to hide the vessel's purpose. The king's agent at Dunkirk, Andrew Frazer, kept the Secretary of State for the Southern Department, Lord Weymouth, well informed about goings on in the French port. Frazer reported regularly on the readiness of the cutter and provided a detailed description of the vessel for Royal Navy officers who would soon be hunting it. Even before Conyngham's release from prison, Lord Stormont knew the Americans intended to have *Greyhound* cruise against British shipping under the command of a naval officer. He communicated this to Vergennes who promised not to let the cutter sail on such a mission. Nevertheless, Stormont was very skeptical of Vergennes' willingness to uphold his promise.

For his part, the French minister sought to avoid trouble by telling Hodge and the commissioners that the cutter would not be allowed to leave port unless the Americans guaranteed that the vessel would sail directly for the United States and not take prizes. Hoping to convince the British of his sincerity, Vergennes reported his actions. Stormont and Weymouth held on to their suspicions, the latter pointing out to his ambassador in France that the Americans knew full well that their continued violation of French neutrality would eventually lead to war between Great Britain and France. Therefore, assur-

The French enjoyed taunting the British by publishing satirical cartoons such as this one showing British ships fleeing Conyngham holding an American naval ensign.

ances meant little as the Americans deliberately abused France's neutral status and would continue to do so as long as the French allowed them to remain. The British Navy ordered warships into the English Channel to guard against a sudden sortie by Conyngham's new vessel.

Unable to provide the guarantee the French were seeking, Hodge enlisted the help of the American commissioners who tried to get Vergennes to change his mind while Hodge worked on getting *Greyhound* ready for sea. The cutter required a larger crew than *Surprize*, and the Americans sought to recruit about 150 men for the new vessel. A number of Americans were part of the new crew, with recent escapees from British prisons adding to those who shipped over from *Surprize*. The majority of the crew appears to have been recruited locally from among the unemployed seamen who hung around the port for just such an opportunity. However, Dunkirk was known as a haven for outlawed smugglers and many of these men joined Conyngham's crew. One British observer characterized them as "a gang of desperadoes." These men, expecting quick booty and uninterested in the laws of maritime

nations, would give Conyngham a great deal of trouble in the weeks ahead.

The American stay in Dunkirk had some exciting moments. Early in July a group of American seamen from Conyngham's cutter ran into a group of English sailors in town. Words were exchanged and before long a scuffle broke out that became quite violent before French authorities broke it up. Two men were seriously wounded. The two sides, not considering the matter settled, secretly agreed to meet outside of the walls of the town the next day. Suspicious, the French officials reported the incident to the military garrison commander who had a group of soldiers standing by. The following day the rival groups of armed sailors clashed, but the French soldiers arrived in time to end the engagement before much violence occurred.

As trouble continued and British protests about the cutter grew, Dunkirk rapidly became an unwelcome place for Conyngham and his men. The American commissioners in Paris sent their secretary, William Carmichael, to Dunkirk to assist Hodge in getting the cutter to sea. The Americans were getting desperate, and with Vergennes holding firm on his demand for security, they hit on an idea. Hodge arranged the sale of *Greyhound* to a man named Richard Allen. With the vessel under new ownership, Hodge (and possibly Carmichael) argued to the officials at Dunkirk that the order preventing the ship from sailing without security no longer applied. The French officials did not examine the sale closely and agreed to allow the cutter to depart. Allen, however, was none other than Gustavus Conyngham himself, and the sale was a fraud.

On 15 July Carmichael gave Gustavus written orders on behalf of the commissioners at Paris to sail directly for the United States without taking prizes in order to avoid offending the Ministry of France. The orders granted an exception if the American found himself short of provisions or attacked by the enemy. In either case, he was allowed to take prizes for his own preservation or to make reprisal for damages received.

Taking advantage of the temporary absence of two British warships that had been watching the port, Conyngham put to sea on the evening of 17 July, officially commissioning his new vessel the Continental Navy cutter *Revenge*. Conyngham had created another set of papers identifying himself as Richard Allen, captain of the North Carolina privateer *Pegasus*. Although Gustavus may have intended to sail for home, he still believed that his primary mission was to cruise against British shipping, and he needed few excuses to invoke the exceptions granted him in his orders.

Success in British Waters

Conyngham took *Revenge* to the northward after leaving Dunkirk, cautiously looking for signs of Royal Navy warships. On the evening of 18 July the lookouts spotted a British frigate, which fired several guns and gave chase. The American captain knew that *Revenge* was no match in a gunnery duel, but the barnacle-encrusted frigate could not keep up with the freshly overhauled, swift cutter, which soon outsailed its opponent. The next day the scenario was repeated with another British frigate, only this time the American vessel passed into the open waters of the North Sea.

Having escaped capture, Captain Conyngham faced

The Continental Navy cutter Revenge *bears down on a merchant vessel in the English Channel.*

the first major test of this independent command. *Revenge* passed several merchant vessels along the busy trade route, and many in the crew became restless, protesting that Conyngham ought not to let such easy prizes get away. The crew's disreputable character revealed itself and, not for the last time, affected the American captain's decision regarding the capture of another ship. Undoubtedly, Gustavus conferred with his officers that evening, and on the following morning declared that *Revenge* would pursue a new course of action. Seizing on the exceptions given in his orders, Gustavus decided to begin a cruise against British shipping.

It is not difficult to see how he reached his conclusion. The nature of command during the Age of Sail forced a ship's captain to rely on his own judgment and resources in fulfilling the spirit of his orders to a far greater degree than is true today. Conyngham's years of experience no doubt left him comfortable with this idea. Furthermore, he had no interest in issues of diplomacy like Lambert Wickes, or in creating a professional officer corps like John Paul Jones. Gustavus did understand the importance of trade to Great Britain, and he believed that his encounter with the British frigates justified his attack on enemy shipping in fulfillment of the larger trust granted to him by his commission in the Continental Navy.

On 20 July *Revenge* met up with a Scottish sloop smuggling gin along the coast of England. After plundering the vessel, the Americans set it on fire, taking the crew as prisoners on board. The next day they cap-

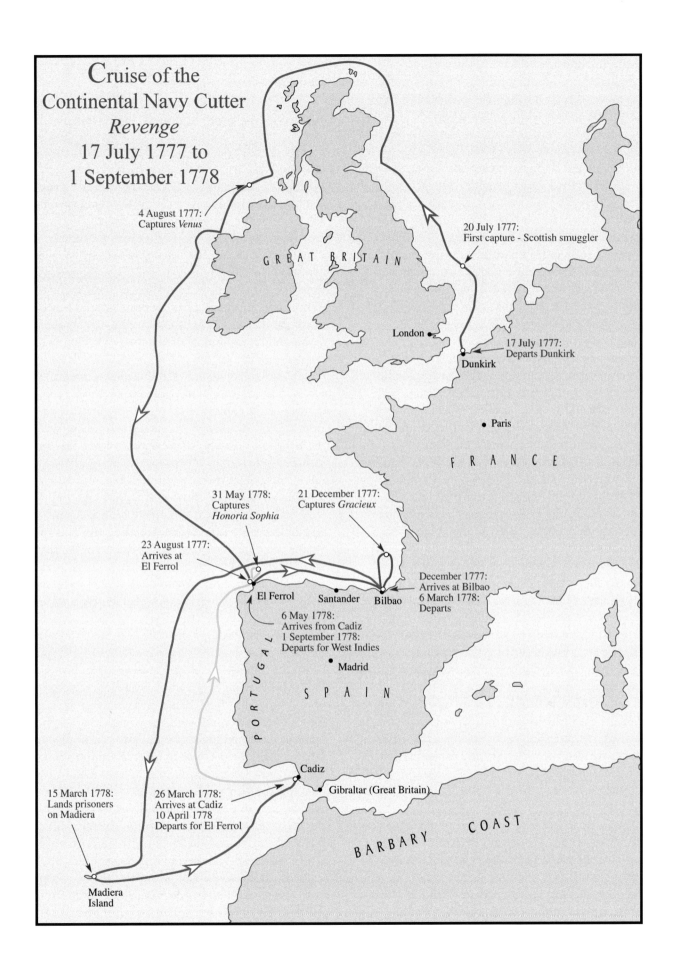

Cruise of the
Continental Navy Cutter
Revenge
17 July 1777 to
1 September 1778

4 August 1777:
Captures *Venus*

20 July 1777:
First capture - Scottish smuggler

GREAT BRITAIN

London

17 July 1777:
Departs Dunkirk

Dunkirk

Paris

FRANCE

31 May 1778:
Captures
Honoria Sophia

21 December 1777:
Captures *Gracieux*

23 August 1777:
Arrives at
El Ferrol

El Ferrol   Santander   Bilbao

December 1777:
Arrives at Bilbao
6 March 1778:
Departs

6 May 1778:
Arrives from Cadiz
1 September 1778:
Departs for West Indies

Madrid

PORTUGAL

SPAIN

Cadiz

15 March 1778:
Lands prisoners
on Madiera

26 March 1778:
Arrives at Cadiz
10 April 1778
Departs for El Ferrol

Gibraltar (Great Britain)

BARBARY   COAST

Madiera
Island

tured the British merchant brig *Northampton*, and Conyngham placed a prize crew of twenty men on board under the command of Benjamin Bailey with orders to take the vessel to Bilbao, Spain. No sooner had he sent Bailey on his way than Gustavus received reports that two more brigs were in sight. *Revenge* set off in pursuit and by that evening had captured both. One, *Maria*, carried no cargo and Conyngham ordered it burned. The American captain decided to ransom the other British brig, *Patty*, for 600 guineas, and set it free after placing the prisoners from his three other prizes on board. Ransoming a prize was an accepted practice whereby a hostage was taken and held until the owner of the vessel paid the amount demanded by the captor. In this case, the owners of *Patty* were to send their payment directly to the American commissioners in Paris.

Conyngham brought *Revenge* north and around Scotland to cruise in the waters thought by Franklin and Deane to contain a large number of vulnerable trading vessels. However, Lambert Wickes' raid into the Irish Sea the previous month had had a profound effect on British trade, as many merchants refused to set sail until the Royal Navy drove the Americans out of local waters. It was not until two weeks after capturing *Patty* that *Revenge* took its next prize, the whaling brig *Venus* on 4 August. Conyngham ordered a prize crew to take the vessel to Martinique in the French West Indies for sale.

After putting his cutter into Broad Haven Bay on the west coast of Ireland to take on fresh water and place prisoners from *Venus* on shore, Conyngham set sail for America or the West Indies. A short time later, *Revenge* ran into a strong gale that severely damaged the rigging and delayed its progress westward. Because of the damage and dwindling provisions, Conyngham realized that he must put into some port in Europe before sailing to America. Gustavus chose to bring the rebel cutter into El Ferrol, Spain, where he arrived on 23 August. He captured the British brig *Black Prince* the day before and sent it into the Spanish port. Conyngham found that his reputation had preceded him.

On 23 July, two days after *Revenge* and *Northampton* parted company, prize master Bailey and his first mate, Francis Mulligan, determined to carry their prize brig into a British port and turn it over to the authorities. They arrived at Great Yarmouth, England, on 26 July and immediately told their story to the Royal Navy officer in charge. News of Conyngham's return to the shipping lanes quickly spread, and by the time he put into El Ferrol, officials there already knew that Richard Allen and Gustavus Conyngham were one and the same.

Spanish Support Sustains Operations

The day after he arrived in Spain, Gustavus sent a letter to Silas Deane indicating his intention to sail for America when repairs to his cutter were completed, but also his willingness to act on his own and "distress the trade of England in another quarter." The American commissioners responded by ordering *Revenge* on a cruise, but leaving management of the campaign to Conyngham himself. The reply was all the self-confident captain needed to hear, and over the next several months Gustavus strengthened his relationships in Spain, which allowed him to maintain his vessel and crew while operating out of the ports of that country.

When he first arrived at El Ferrol, Conyngham received a warm welcome from the Spanish governor general of the province, Don Felix O'Neille. The two immediately developed a working relationship. Over the next four months, O'Neille permitted *Revenge* to refit and provision in his ports, as well as allowing the sale of American prizes. On one occasion he even intervened to ensure the sale of a prize taken by Conyngham. O'Neille also assisted Gustavus in reclaiming deserting sailors, including British subjects, which caused a good deal of tension between Spain and Great Britain.

One deserter, Englishman John Jordan, who had enlisted on board *Revenge*, fled the vessel on 18 November, while the cutter was at Corunna, and ran to the British consul, Herman Katencamp, complaining of ill treatment. The British official placed him on board an English merchant vessel ready to leave port. Discovering what happened, Conyngham protested to one of O'Neille's lieutenants, who issued a stern warning to Katencamp not to make trouble. When the Spanish governor general returned the next day, he informed the British consul that the matter was closed. Nevertheless, on the night of 20 November, Conyngham ordered five men from *Revenge*, accompanied by two of O'Neille's Spanish soldiers, to board the merchant vessel. The boarding party forcibly removed Jordan and returned him to the American cutter. Katencamp delivered a strong protest, but O'Neille dragged the matter out for nearly a month until orders came from Madrid to give Jordan back to the British.

Even more important to *Revenge*'s success was the assistance given by two powerful Spanish commercial

AUGUSTATUS KUNINGAM

Captain Gustavus Conyngham ready for action.

The American "Navies" of the Revolutionary War

Unlike today, the Continental Navy during the American Revolution did not enjoy a monopoly in American military operations on the sea. The Continental Navy represented only one part of the American naval effort that also included "Washington's Navy," state navies, and privateers.

The Continental Army had its own naval service (often called "Washington's Navy") that predated the Continental Navy. Even after the Continental Navy came into existence in late 1775, army officers continued to command vessels in Long Island Sound, off Massachusetts, and, most notably, on Lake Champlain where General Benedict Arnold scored one of America's greatest naval successes at the Battle of Valcour Island in 1776. Although Arnold's fleet was destroyed, he was able to turn back a British invasion from Canada, buying time for the Americans to mount a successful defense the next year when they forced a British army to surrender at Saratoga, New York.

The states, too, operated their own independent navies. With the exceptions of New Jersey and Delaware, each of the original thirteen states operated at least one armed ship during the Revolution. While the navy of no one state was as large as the Continental Navy, the total number of state navy vessels greatly exceeded the number of vessels under control of Congress. Generally, state navy vessels were smaller than their Continental Navy counterparts. Their size reflected the fact that the states had fewer resources than had the Continental Congress and that the primary mission of the state navies was to protect the seaports, coasts, and trade of the states. Adapted for moving in and out of shallow harbors, bays, and rivers, smaller-sized craft proved better suited to accomplish this mission. The navy of only one state, Massachusetts, had more craft designed for deep water than for inshore work. Many state navy vessels did, however, act in concert with Continental Navy ships by cruising, escorting merchantmen, and even participating in joint opera-

tions, such as the attack on Penobscot, Maine, in 1779. The Continental Navy, with its bigger ships and closer supervision by Congress, performed missions that were different from, and less locally focused than, those the state navies performed.

By far, privateering represented the greatest part of the American naval effort. Privateers were privately owned, armed vessels that operated in time of war against the commerce of the enemy. They ranged from private vessels devoted exclusively to warlike operations to armed trading vessels authorized to capture enemy ships. Such vessels operated independently, though they were commissioned by the government through formal documents called letters of marque and reprisal that licensed them to take prizes. In return, the owners of such vessels were required to post bonds to ensure the good behavior of their privateers. When a privateer captured an enemy vessel (a prize), it returned the captured ship to port where, if normal procedures were followed, a hearing was held in a special court (the Admiralty Court) to decide the legitimacy of the capture. If the court ruled that the prize was legitimate, the ship and its cargo were sold and the net proceeds (the prize money) split among the privateers' owners and its captain and crew according to a formula established by contract before the privateer sailed.

Since Congress allowed Continental Navy captains and crews to keep only one-half of the value of many of the prizes they captured, privateering could be much more lucrative than regular naval service for the average sailor. Continental Navy captains constantly complained of the difficulty they had

The American privateer Hyder Ali *capturing HMS* General Monk; *privateers were commerce raiders and rarely challenged British warships.*

recruiting and retaining men in the face of competition from privateers.

Until the Declaration of Paris in 1856 outlawed privateering, all nations engaged in privateering, and privateers were especially prevalent during the American Revolution. It is estimated that Americans sent out between two thousand and three thousand privateers to prey on British commerce. The British, too, commissioned privateers and, though fewer in numbers than their American counterparts, these privateers on average were larger and better armed. Assessing the effects of American privateers on the war, one American modern naval historian has written: "Valuable service to the country was rendered by the privateers, and they contributed in a large degree to the naval defense, and so to the fortunate outcome of the war. On the other hand, the system was subject to abuses and was in many ways detrimental to the regular naval service." Another has commented that, despite taking more than two thousand enemy prizes, American privateers damaged Britain's "pride far more than its pocketbook" and evoked a "cry of rage rather than of pain."

While none of these elements in the American naval effort could or did succeed alone, in tandem they contributed to the sapping of the British will to fight that in the end gained America its independence.

houses, Lagoanere & Company at El Ferrol and Corunna, and Joseph Gardoqui & Sons at Bilbao. These merchants had long done business with the American colonists, and they were eager to support the new nation in a cause with which they sympathized. They helped Conyngham sell his prizes and provision his crew. Gustavus used the American government's share of the prize money to pay his crew's wages and refit *Revenge*. The commissioners at Paris used some of the prize money to purchase, through the Gardoquis, weapons and goods for use by the Continental Army. Conyngham had accumulated so much money with Lagonanere & Company that American Commissioner John Adams was able to draw $3,000 from the account for traveling expenses when visiting Corunna in February 1780.

Revenge captured four vessels while operating out of El Ferrol and Corunna during the fall of 1777. As Conyngham's notoriety grew, the British ambassador and his consuls put increasing pressure on the Spanish Court to take stronger action in prohibiting the rebel cutter or its prizes from entering port and abusing the country's neutral status. The Spanish Minister of State, Conde de Floridablanca, seemed content to allow the merchant houses and local authorities to help the Americans as long as they simply harassed the British. As troublesome as the British diplomats were, Conyngham's own actions led to his unpopularity in Madrid and forced the Royal Court to intervene to have him banned from Spainish ports.

During the middle of December 1777, Gustavus shifted his base of operations to Bilbao. On 21 December *Revenge* stopped the French brig *Gracieux*, bound from London to Spain with a valuable cargo of woolen goods. Conyngham considered letting the vessel go, but his crew, driven by the desire for prize money, insisted that their captain capture the brig. Knowing British captains had taken French and Spanish ships carrying American-owned goods, Gustavus gave in to his men's demand and sent the vessel into port with a prize crew, intending to sell the cargo on the basis that it was British property.

This act outraged Spanish officials, who threw the prize crew into jail and confiscated the brig. The Royal Court responded by sending a strongly worded complaint to the American commissioners in Paris, and by insisting that Conyngham be expelled from Spain's ports. The American commissioners reprimanded Gustavus for taking the French brig and left no room for misunderstanding that he was to capture only British-owned vessels and withdraw his claim on *Gracieux*'s cargo. Conyngham angrily responded that

"damned policy" would not satisfy sailors, and that he was being criticized for doing exactly what British captains had done on many occasions. Although *Revenge*'s crew of mostly European seamen and smugglers pushed their captain to make captures under questionable circumstances, he was not unsympathetic to their desires.

While *Revenge* remained at Bilbao, Gustavus traveled to San Sebastián where the Spanish held the prize crew prisoner. He spent most of January and February at the small port, arguing for the release of his crewmen as well as *Gracieux*'s cargo until he received orders to drop the claim. Frustrated but not discouraged, Conyngham began to feel the pressure from Spanish officials, and he departed Bilbao on 6 March 1778, once again intending to sail for Martinique.

On 10 March, just before leaving European waters, *Revenge* encountered the brigantine *Peace & Harmony* with a cargo of oranges bound for London. Conyngham took the vessel as a prize, but in order to avoid the problems with the use of Spanish ports, he ordered it to Massachusetts. The American cutter captured the brigantine *Betsy* the next day, and on 12 March took the snow *Fanny*, both of which he sent to Massachusetts. Meeting with unexpected success, Gustavus again demonstrated flexibility in fulfilling his orders, and returned to his first priority of attacking British trade where it was vulnerable. He placed his prisoners on the island of Madeira and sailed for the Straits of Gibraltar to test his luck against British merchant vessels returning home from the Mediterranean.

Revenge fell in with the tender to the British frigate HMS *Enterprize* on 20 March, and Conyngham decided to set the vessel ablaze. Four days later the American cutter encountered a feistier opponent. Late that afternoon a lookout sighted a ship-rigged vessel coming toward them, and *Revenge*'s captain called the men to quarters to man the ten guns on deck. The ship turned out to be the letter of marque *Hope*, mounting sixteen guns. The British captain initially mistook the American cutter for a merchant vessel and fired a warning shot to persuade the captain to stop. Gustavus slyly allowed the British ship to come alongside *Revenge*, and with a shout ordered his crew to run out their guns and give their enemies a broadside. The blast caught the British by surprise and wounded their captain, who surrendered his vessel after the Americans fired a second broadside at point blank range. At that point British frigates HMS *Enterprize* and HMS *Levant* appeared on the horizon, and Conyngham hastily placed a prize crew on board the new capture hoping that they could get away into the approaching

Conyngham prepared his crew for a fight with a British warship by regularly drilling them in the use of the ship's guns.

darkness. The American cutter outdistanced its pursuers in the falling wind as the crew took to the oars and disappeared into the night. *Enterprize* recaptured *Hope* the next morning and escorted it into the British base at Gibraltar.

Conyngham brought *Revenge* into the nearby Spanish port of Cadiz on 26 March and, much to the embarrassment of the British captain still awaiting permission to enter the port, was immediately granted access by the local governor. After paying his respects to this Spanish official, Gustavus visited the offices of Le Couteulx and Co., a commercial house supportive of the American cause. The company worked with the American commissioners in Paris to ship needed goods to the United States, and the merchants readily agreed to refit and provision *Revenge*.

Receiving new orders, Conyngham sailed from Cadiz on 10 April to continue cruising off the coasts of Spain and Portugal. He took four prizes during the next month, putting into Corunna with his last capture, the brig *Maria*, on 6 May to refit and clean the cutter's bottom. The Spanish governor received the American captain warmly and secretly arranged for the sale of *Maria*'s cargo, leaving the profits on deposit with Lagoanere & Co. Regretfully, the governor informed Gustavus that he had strict orders to make sure the American left port as soon as *Revenge*'s refit was complete. Word of this spread to the cutter's cantankerous crew, who decided to take advantage of the situation by demanding that they be paid their prize money up to date or else they would leave the ship. As most of these men signed on for one cruise at a time and recruiting in the Spanish port was forbidden, Conyngham had little choice but to give in.

Revenge departed Corunna on 20 May, intercepting the Swedish brig *Honoria Sophia* on the last day of the month. The brig carried a British-owned cargo of dry goods from London to Teneriffe in the Canary Islands. After the incident with the *Gracieux*, Conyngham knew he must let the neutral vessel go, but his prize-hungry crew would not hear of it. Gustavus's trusted friend and first lieutenant, John Beach, was no longer on board, and the American captain suddenly found himself alone, facing a crew precariously close to mutiny. Conyngham stepped aside as his men sent a prize crew to the Swedish brig with orders to carry it into an American port. For their part, the crew signed a statement accepting responsibility for their action.

Conyngham's attempt to distance himself from the capture was in vain as news of the outrage swept through the Spanish royal court where the attitude hardened against the American captain. When he

returned to Corunna from a long and fruitless cruise on 20 August, the usually friendly governor denied him entry. Gustavus sailed along the coast to a nearby inlet where he met with Spanish friends (probably from Lagoanere & Co.), who helped him clean and refit *Revenge*.

The capture of *Honoria Sophia* forced the American commissioners in Paris to exercise major diplomatic damage control. They repudiated Conyngham's action and assured foreign representatives that if found guilty, he would be punished. Gustavus had clearly lost his support in Europe and the time had arrived for *Revenge* to sail west.

Cruising the Caribbean

Conyngham left Spain on 1 September 1778 and arrived at the French island of Martinique in the Caribbean Sea on 9 October. Gustavus reported to William Bingham, the American Continental agent at the port of St. Pierre, who had authority to give the Continental Navy captain orders related to operations in the eastern Caribbean. Bingham had *Revenge* fitted out for a cruise and helped Conyngham recruit replacements for his crew. The large American cutter set sail on 26 October from St. Pierre, carrying instructions from the Continental agent to attack British trade in the region.

For more than two weeks *Revenge* worked its way north, against the prevailing winds and toward the smaller British-controlled islands. Finally, on 13 November, Conyngham had his busiest day of the war. The cutter first captured the sloop *Two Friends* carrying casks of water. Gustavus sent the vessel back to Martinique, but a British privateer recaptured it before it reached the French island. The Americans then encountered two small schooners, which were taken and sent into St. Eustatius and sold. Toward the end of the day, *Revenge* encountered one of the many British privateers that infested the Caribbean, the schooner *Admiral Barrington*, mounting six 2-pounders and fourteen swivels. The swift cutter easily ran down the schooner, and the British could not hope to survive a gun duel with the better-armed *Revenge*. After the privateer struck its colors, Conyngham put a prize crew on board with the intention of having it operate in conjunction with his vessel. He apparently changed his mind the next day and sent *Admiral Barrington* to Martinique before sailing *Revenge* into St. Eustatius to take on food and water.

One day after setting sail on 16 November, the Continental Navy cutter encountered the British pri-

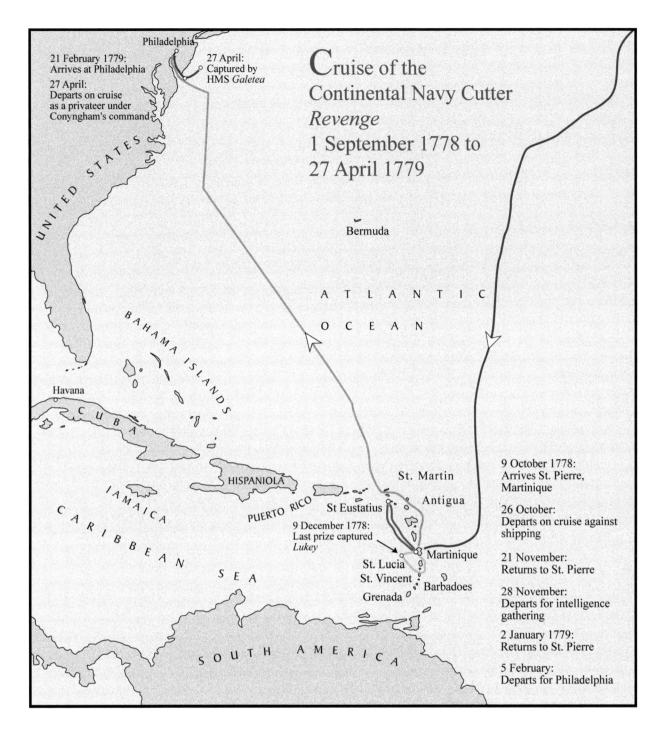

Cruise of the
Continental Navy Cutter
Revenge
1 September 1778 to
27 April 1779

21 February 1779:
Arrives at Philadelphia

27 April:
Departs on cruise
as a privateer under
Conyngham's command

27 April:
Captured by
HMS *Galetea*

Philadelphia

UNITED STATES

ATLANTIC

OCEAN

Bermuda

BAHAMA ISLANDS

Havana

CUBA

HISPANIOLA

JAMAICA

PUERTO RICO

CARIBBEAN

SEA

St Eustatius

St. Martin

Antigua

9 December 1778:
Last prize captured
Lukey

St. Lucia

St. Vincent

Grenada

Martinique

Barbadoes

SOUTH AMERICA

9 October 1778:
Arrives St. Pierre,
Martinique

26 October:
Departs on cruise against
shipping

21 November:
Returns to St. Pierre

28 November:
Departs for intelligence
gathering

2 January 1779:
Returns to St. Pierre

5 February:
Departs for Philadelphia

vateer brig *Loyalist*, with fifty men and mounting ten 3-pounders and fourteen swivels. The British captain decided to put up a fight, but the heavier broadsides of *Revenge* subdued its opponent. Conyngham brought the privateer brig back with him to Martinique where he arrived on 21 November.

He left St. Pierre on another cruise one week later with additional instructions from Bingham to communicate intelligence on British movements to the French fleet. *Revenge* took its last prize, the brig *Lukey*, on 9 December 1778, which was sold at Martinique. Conyngham sailed in company with the French fleet

in the Caribbean from 15 to 29 December, keeping a safe distance as French and British warships sparred off St. Lucia. The Continental Navy cutter returned to Martinique for repairs on 2 January 1779.

Bingham decided to use *Revenge* to carry a needed shipment of arms to the United States. Conyngham left St. Pierre with his vessel on 5 February, arriving in Philadelphia, Pennsylvania, on 21 February after an uneventful voyage. Thus, nineteen months after being commissioned into the service of the United States, *Revenge* arrived at a home port. Gustavus was greeted by news of trouble that had been brewing there the

Mill Prison, Plymouth, England, where the British kept many of their captured American sailors.

past few months. Former crewmembers of the cutter (mostly from prize crews), led by ship's surgeon Josiah Smith, filed a memorial with the Continental Congress complaining of Conyngham's conduct, particularly regarding the timely distribution of prize money. Congress started an investigation by requesting financial accounts and letters of instruction from the commercial houses that had dealings with the Continental Navy captain and the prizes of *Revenge*. Conyngham himself was summoned to provide an account of his cruises. It was not long before the investigators realized that the affair was too complicated to find resolution during the war, and on 12 March the cash-strapped Congress ordered the sale of the cutter at public auction in Philadelphia.

In Irons

A firm of Philadelphia merchants, who intended to use the vessel as a privateer, outbid the competition for *Revenge*. One of those outbid at the auction was the State of Pennsylvania, which hoped to use the armed cutter to protect commerce on the Delaware River. The new owners agreed to allow the state to charter the vessel for about two weeks with Conyngham as its captain. When the charter expired in April, Gustavus put to sea in command of *Revenge*, once again on a cruise against British shipping. It was a unique arrangement as Conyngham sailed under his commission in the Continental Navy even though the cutter was now a private vessel with its captain a part owner.

Unfortunately, the raider's return to the shipping lanes met with disaster almost immediately. As *Revenge* rounded the Delaware capes and sailed for New York the large cutter encountered two enemy privateers on 27 April. Itching for an engagement, Conyngham pursued them close inshore where they led *Revenge* into the very teeth of the frigate HMS *Galatea*. The Americans attempted to escape but, having come too close to the British warship and its heavier armament, were forced to surrender. Taking him to British-controlled New York, Conyngham's captors placed him in irons on board a prison ship and threatened him with execution for piracy under the pretense that he had operated without a commission when he took the Harwich packet in May 1777 while in command of *Surprize*.

On 12 June 1779, Gustavus wrote a letter to his wife, Ann, telling her of his predicament, the uncivil way that he was being treated, and the British plans to send him immediately to Great Britain. Ann petitioned Congress on 17 July to take immediate action, fearing that "the delay of a single hour may fix my husband's fate for ever." Seventy-nine friends, relatives, and businessmen in Philadelphia revealed how popular Gustavus was in his hometown by adding their voices to Ann's, calling for a swift response. That very day Congress drafted a letter to the British naval commander at New York claiming Conyngham as a citizen and officer in the service of the Untied States, and demanding his proper treatment. Furthermore, unless Congress received a satisfactory answer by the first of August, they would select a British officer in custody to receive similar treatment and share the fate of the American captain.

His captors kept Gustavus in heavy irons and on

meager rations during the voyage across the Atlantic and for the few weeks that he was confined in Pendennis Castle at Falmouth. Apparently reacting to a notice that a British naval officer was in irons awaiting execution should Conyngham be put to death, the British Admiralty transferred the American to Mill Prison in Plymouth, where he joined 190 fellow countrymen eligible for exchange.

Nevertheless, the restless Irish-American refused to bide his time until exchanged for a British prisoner. Gustavus made two unsuccessful attempts to escape—one time walking out the front gate in the dress of a visiting doctor. He succeeded on his third attempt, along with fifty-three others, on 3 November, by tunneling under the prison wall. Making his way to London, Conyngham contacted an American sympathizer who helped him get across the English Channel to Holland. There he placed himself under the orders of Captain John Paul Jones while waiting for instructions from Benjamin Franklin.

Told to remain with Jones for the time being, Conyngham accompanied him and his small squadron as it ran past the British blockade on 27 December and began a short cruise against enemy trade in the English Channel. Jones eventually took his ships to Corunna, Spain, where Gustavus decided to part company and return to America on board a merchant vessel. As luck would have it, the British captured the vessel en route on 17 March 1780, and Conyngham soon found himself back at Mill Prison.

This time he remained a prisoner for more than a year, much of the time in poor health. He got word of his situation to American merchants at Lorient, France, who sent money to help sustain him. Ann Conyngham traveled to Lorient to be closer to her husband when he was released or escaped. Very few American privateers operated in European waters during this time so there were no prisoners taken that could be exchanged for U.S. citizens suffering at Mill Prison. With little hope of being released, Gustavus determined to escape and finally succeeded in June 1781.

Although no doubt happy to be reunited with Ann in France, Gustavus felt greatly concerned about his fellow Americans languishing in British prisons. Exchange was the only hope for many of these men, and Conyngham hoped to supply the necessary British prisoners through another cruise, this time in the 24-gun ship *Layona* being built at Lorient. Unfortunately, the French had other uses for this vessel, and the American's plans fell through. Disappointed, Conyngham returned to Philadelphia on board the ship *Hannibal* carrying a number of recent escapees.

Condemned to Obscurity

Gustavus tried to return to service after arriving home, but the fast-dwindling Continental Navy had little use for another unemployed captain. The fact that his original commissions had been taken from him did not help his efforts. Franklin provided a letter certifying Conyngham's status, which the naval officer included in an October 1782 memorial to Congress asking for recognition of his rank so that he could receive the pay and prize money due him. It was not until 5 January 1784, almost a year after the war ended, that a committee formed to investigate his petition responded. Because he did not receive his commission directly from Congress, he was not given a rank in relation to other Continental Navy captains. Furthermore, the committee announced that the commissions provided by the American commissioners at Paris were intended only for temporary expeditions, and Conyngham's request was denied.

Despite this rebuff Gustavus continued to serve his country willingly in time of war while also seeking recognition for his service in the American Revolution. During the Quasi-War with France (1798–1801) he made several cruises in the privateer brig *Maria*, meeting with little success. He attempted to get to sea again during the War of 1812, but his advanced age and failing health forced him to give up. For the remainder of his life Gustavus continued to petition Congress for compensation for services rendered the country while in command of the Continental Navy cutter *Revenge*. His efforts ended only with his death in Philadelphia on 27 November 1819.

Gustavus Conyngham held to his strategic vision throughout his career in the Continental Navy. Great Britain's trade at sea was its lifeline, and that trade was vulnerable to attack by even a small naval force like that of the Americans. Conyngham used his experience, intelligence, and imagination to keep his command operational so that he could hurl it again and again at the enemy's weak points. He possessed command abilities unusual in a naval officer. He could gain the cooperation of government officials and achieve victory with a greedy and disreputable crew. Merchants on both sides of the Atlantic respected and assisted him, and rallied to his side when he needed support. Conyngham took thirty-one prizes while in command of *Surprize* and *Revenge*, more than any other American naval officer did in the Revolutionary War. His legacy to the United States Navy is one of determination, imagination, and success.

John Paul Jones

By Dennis M. Conrad

John Paul Jones personifies the fighting spirit and the never-say-die attitude of the United States Navy. This spirit was never more evident than at the Battle off Flamborough Head, one of the most desperate seafights in naval history and the most famous engagement involving an American vessel fought during the American Revolution.

In September 1779, Jones served as captain of *Bonhomme Richard*, an old converted merchant vessel, and commanded a "fleet" of three smaller warships in the waters off Scotland and northern England when he encountered a British convoy carrying naval stores to England from the Baltic Sea region. Acting as an escort to this convoy were two British warships. The largest of these warships, which Jones engaged, was *Serapis*, a 44-gun vessel—though at the time carrying fifty guns—with a crew of 284. A ship of that size and firepower occupied a place in the eighteenth-century Royal Navy equivalent to a cruiser in its twentieth-century counterpart. From the battle's onset, *Bonhomme Richard* was at a disadvantage fighting a ship with superior firepower and maneuverability. Moreover, an accident that occurred early in the engagement greatly increased the odds against an American victory. On the second broadside fired by *Bonhomme Richard*, two of its biggest guns exploded. (At least one expert believes only one gun may have exploded, but that two neighboring guns were dismounted by the blast.) In a memoir that he later penned, Jones wrote that many of the officers and men working those guns, "who had been selected as the best of the crew," were killed, wounded, "or so frightened that none of them was of any use during the remainder of the engagement." This accident completely silenced *Bonhomme Richard*'s biggest guns and left the ship vulnerable to being pounded to pieces by *Serapis*.

A portrait of John Paul Jones thought to portray him accurately.

Understanding immediately that it would be suicidal to continue to trade broadsides with *Serapis*, Jones by superior seamanship moved *Bonhomme Richard* close to the enemy ship, allowing his crew to use grapples and lines to secure *Bonhomme Richard* to it, thus negating some of the advantages enjoyed by *Serapis*. Even with the ships locked together, however, the British gunners continued to fire into *Bonhomme Richard* until the hull and lower decks of the American ship were so battered that it resembled more a raft than a fighting ship. In fact, the British gunners

William Gilkerson

Continental Navy ship Bonhomme Richard.

wreaked such devastation with their broadsides that they had to reposition their guns continually or their cannonballs would pass through *Bonhomme Richard* without hitting anything solid.

As the sea poured in through the holes punched in its hull by British cannonballs, the hold of the ship filled with water. As the long battle neared its climax, *Bonhomme Richard* lay half submerged and was kept afloat only because the master at arms released one hundred British prisoners who were told to man the pumps and pump for their lives or the vessel would sink and they would drown. Even their efforts could not keep pace with the incoming sea. In short, the American ship was sinking.

As if this situation were not dire enough, fires raged both aloft in the sails and rigging and below decks. In fact, fighting at times ceased so the crews of both vessels could combat these out-of-control blazes. Finally, the continued pounding inflicted by *Serapis* had left half of Jones' crew dead or wounded.

At this point in the battle, the senior warrant officer of *Bonhomme Richard* and the ship's carpenter, unable to see their captain or the first lieutenant and assuming both were dead, decided to surrender their sinking, burning ship. They called for a ceasefire and ran to haul down the ship's pendant at the head of the mainmast—the signal that an eighteenth-century ship was giving up the fight. Hearing their calls for surrender, an enraged Jones drew his pistols and ran at them, shouting, "shoot them, kill them!" The two would-be

Right, Continental Navy ship Bonhomme Richard *versus* HMS Serapis, *early in the battle. Below,* Bonhomme Richard *versus* Serapis, *later in the battle after Jones' crew grappled* Serapis.

Though the odds against victory remained formidable, Jones' will to win reinvigorated his crew.

surrenderers abandoned their attempt to lower the ship's pendant and turned to flee when they spied Jones approaching them. Jones, finding his pistols unloaded, hurled his empty guns at the carpenter, the slower of the two fleeing men, striking him on the head and knocking him unconscious. The captain of the British warship, who heard the calls for surrender, yelled across to the Jones, "Have you struck? Do you call for Quarter?" Jones then replied, "I have not yet begun to fight,"—words that have defined the American navy ever since. With that, the battle continued.

Jones' fighting spirit and determination were contagious. Though the odds against victory remained formidable, Jones' will to win reinvigorated his crew. They renewed the battle "with double fury" and succeeded in repelling a British boarding party that attempted to capture the American vessel just after the

John Paul Jones shown shooting a sailor who is attempting to strike the colors of the Bonhomme Richard; *this is a wild exaggeration of what actually happened.*

surrender incident. The key moment of the battle then occurred. A Scottish seaman serving in *Bonhomme Richard* climbed down from the top of the mainmast, moved along a spar to a point above *Serapis'* decks and began to throw the eighteenth-century equivalent of hand grenades onto the deck of the enemy. One of these "grenades" rolled down a partially opened hatch and landed near cartridges that had been stacked along the portside guns of Serapis. Because of the position of the two ships, these guns were not in action and these spare cartridges were piled behind them. The grenade's explosion ignited these cartridges, which in turn ignited other cartridges on the gun deck creating a flash-fire, which had a devastatingly horrible effect in the cramped gun deck filled with men and officers. Twenty crewmen died instantly and another thirty were badly injured. Several of these men—their clothes burned off, their skin seared, and their hair on fire—

Did Jones actually say, "I have not yet begun to fight"?

When Captain Richard Pearson of the *Serapis* asked Jones, "Have you struck? Do you call for Quarter?" or, in other words, was Jones prepared to give up the fight and surrender his ship, Jones, according to most accounts, replied, "I have not yet begun to fight." There is, however, some question whether those were Jones' actual words. Richard Dale, Jones' first lieutenant during the battle, first credited him with that immortal phrase. Dale would normally be considered an excellent source but his recollection of Jones' words came forty-six years after the battle when the then retired sixty-five-year-old commodore recounted them to John H. Sherburne, an early biographer of Jones'. Most accounts written immediately after the battle record Jones' words as, "I may sink, but I'm damned if I'll strike" or a very similar phrase.

RICHARD DALE ESQ.

late of the United States Navy.

Richard Dale, above, pictured as a U.S. Navy captain; he was the source for what Jones is reported to have said. Nathaniel Fanning, left, who served as midshipmen under Jones gave a different version of what Jones said.

Such words according to one student of the battle are a "simple direct answer, to a simple direct question." Another eyewitness, Ensign Nathaniel Fanning, later recalled Jones' words to be, "Ay, ay, we'll do that [that is, haul down the pendant of the *Bonhomme Richard*] when we can fight no longer, but we shall see yours come down first; for you must know, that Yankees do not haul down their colours till they are fairly beaten."

While observers do not agree on Jones' exact words, all recall Jones' determination to continue the struggle and the iron will he demonstrated at this crisis in the battle.

jumped out of the ship's gun ports into the sea. With this disaster, the big guns of *Serapis* fell silent.

When news of the disaster was conveyed to the captain, Richard Pearson, he decided to surrender and save his remaining crew from slaughter. Calling for quarter, he personally made his way to the rear of the warship and hauled down the battle ensign. Thus ended the three-and-one-half-hour battle. Jones and his crew had prevailed and had captured the enemy's vessel, which was fortunate since the badly damaged *Bonhomme Richard* sank shortly after the battle. Against long odds and a formidable foe, they had achieved a remarkable victory.

Making his Way: Jones' Youth

While Jones' actions and fighting spirit in the battle off Flamborough Head, the most notable of his career, established him as one of our country's greatest naval heroes, his entire life can be instructive. John Paul Jones was born John Paul on 6 July 1747 at Kirkbean, Kirkcudbright, Scotland, on the shores of Solway Firth. He was the fifth child in his family. His father, also named John, served as the gardener at Arbigland House, an estate at Kirkbean. While not poor, the Pauls were decidedly working class. Some of John Paul Jones' early biographers refused to accept his humble origins and instead insisted that he was the illegitimate son of the Third Earl of Selkirk. According to American historian Samuel Eliot Morison, this story of Jones' "hidden nobility" is the product of "a type of snobbery which insists that every great man who makes a stir in the world (such as Shakespeare, Columbus and Lincoln) must be either a nobleman in disguise or a man of left-handed aristocratic lineage." In truth, Jones was a working class boy who over-came class prejudice and succeeded in a world dominated by the rich and powerful.

Left, sailors and marines whose fire from the tops of Bonhomme Richard *was instrumental in defeating* Serapis. *Captain Sir Richard Pearson, right, commander of HMS* Serapis *whom Jones defeated, but who was knighted in recognition of his conduct during the battle.*

In 1761, at the age of thirteen John Paul became a sailor. Since he lacked "connections," the young man began his career as an apprentice mariner. As an apprentice, he committed himself to seven years' service to John Younger, a merchant operating out of an English port near where John Paul had been raised. His first voyage took John Paul to Fredericksburg, Virginia, where he visited his older brother, a tailor who had earlier immigrated to America. A number of voyages between England, the West Indies, and the Chesapeake followed until 1764 when Younger went bankrupt and released John Paul from his apprenticeship. Young Jones then worked on ships operating in the African slave trade, which recent studies have indi-

The birthplace and childhood home of John Paul Jones.

cated was the most dangerous and least desirable of berths for sailors. Jones could not abide what he called that "abominable trade." Even though unhappy in his position, he made the most of it, and in 1768 when the twenty-one year old Paul left the slaving vessel *Two Friends*, he was its chief mate. Separating from *Two Friends* in Jamaica, John Paul took passage home on a brig, *John*, and when both the captain and chief mate died of disease on the brig's voyage to Scotland, John Paul, being the only person aboard who could navigate, assumed command and brought the vessel and its crew of seven safely to Kirkcudbright.

The owners of *John*, pleased with John Paul's performance, asked him to continue as captain and for the next two years he served as master and selling agent for *John*, making several voyages between Scotland and the West Indies. By 1772, he had graduated to command of *Betsy*, a large square-rigged merchant vessel.

Through personal initiative, merit, force of character, and luck, John Paul had in the space of a few years risen from ship's boy to become a captain. Unlike many of his contemporaries, his opportunities were not provided to him; he made his own way and at a young age had achieved much.

John Paul's life took a dramatic turn in 1773 as a result of his ferocious temper. One of the seamen on *Betsy*, to whom Jones later referred simply as the ring-leader, challenged Paul's authority and fomented a mutiny when the ship arrived at the West Indian island of Tobago. Jones confronted the ringleader with a sword, intending, as he later asserted, to intimidate the sailor into obedience. According to Jones, the ringleader then went berserk, picked up a piece of wood and came at Jones, who defended himself with his sword against repeated blows. Finally Jones, in self-defense, stabbed his attacker, killing him. If Jones' account is accurate, his subsequent actions seem strange. A few days after the incident, Jones fled Tobago, traveled "Incog[nito]" to America, changed his name, and "reinvented" himself. Either Jones' rendition of the events leading to the sailor's death were not as he later portrayed them or the killing of the man, a Tobagoan, though justifiable, so inflamed the local population that Jones and his friends feared that he could never receive justice and therefore must flee.

His ability to recover from what he himself later called "that great Misfortune of my Life" was an important turning point in Jones' career. He arrived in America, which, he later wrote, had long been his "favorite Country," intending to settle there permanently and "quit the Sea Service" using money owed him as a mer-

chant captain to "purchase some small tracts of Land." Whether or not he genuinely desired to abandon the sea cannot be known; however, events quickly overtook him and propelled him back to a maritime career.

Jones Joins the Continental Navy

Jones arrived in America just as the crisis in relations between the American colonies and England came to a climax, culminating in fighting between British soldiers and colonial militiamen at Lexington and Concord in Massachusetts in April 1775. Reacting to these clashes, the Continental Congress created a Continental army and navy. Officers were needed to staff this new navy. Responding quickly, Jones went to Philadelphia to offer his services. In addition to needing a job, Jones had other motives for volunteering. As he later wrote, he had made "the Art of War by Sea" his "Study" and had been "fond of a Navy from my boyish

John Paul Jones' commission as a captain in the Continental Navy.

continued on page 54

Guns and Gun Crews

Sailing warships were floating gun platforms. Seamanship in battle was the art of putting your vessel in a position that allowed you to fire the greatest number of guns at the enemy while minimizing the number of guns the enemy could bring to bear on your vessel. Close action was the order of the day and speed of firing was more highly prized than accuracy. Gun crews, numbering as many as nine men, were trained to reload rapidly and reposition a gun for firing. Some captains did not even have their men take target practice.

Guns of the period were classified by the weight of the round shot, or ball, fired by it. The largest guns on triple-decker men of war were 42-pounders, though 32-pounders were more common. Smaller vessels, such as frigates, carried 12-pounder guns. These 12-pounders varied in length from seven to nine feet and in weight from 2,100 to 3,700 pounds. Ships of the time also carried 6-, 8-, and 9-pounders. These guns ranged in size from six feet to eight feet, six inches long and weighed from 1,700 to 2,200 pounds. Round shot was most commonly used to punch holes in the hull of the opposing vessel. Other kinds of shot included bar shot and chain shot. The former, shaped like a barbell, and the latter—two small balls held together by a short chain—were designed to destroy rigging. Grapeshot, cylindrical canvas bags filled with nine smaller iron balls lashed tightly together, could be used against rigging or against an enemy's crew. For a 12-pounder, each of the nine grapeshot balls weighed one pound; for a 6-pounder, each weighed eight ounces. Canister shot, designed as an antipersonnel weapon, was akin to oversized shotgun shells and filled with

musket balls.

A ship's gun in this period consisted merely of a tube closed at one end. At the closed end was a chamber where powder was placed for firing. Prior to action, loose gunpowder was packed into cartridges made of paper or flannel cloth. These cartridges, for obvious reasons, were stored in the interior of the ship and, ideally, were brought up individually during the battle by young boys called "powder monkeys." A cartridge was placed in the gun first and rammed down so that it fit snugly against the closed end of the chamber. After the cartridge was inserted, a ball was put in followed by a wad. This wad was made of old rope or "junk," and was used to hold the cannonball in place. One school of thought held that placing an additional wad between the cartridge and the ball would improve the ballistics of the gun. As the first broadside fired by a vessel was widely considered to be its most accurate and most effective, the guns were often loaded with double shot, which meant a second ball and another wad were added. Both the *Serapis* and the *Bonhomme Richard* opened the battle off Flamborough Head using double shot. After the first volley or two, when speed became more critical, the second ball and additional wad were eliminated.

The gun crew, which numbered from six to nine

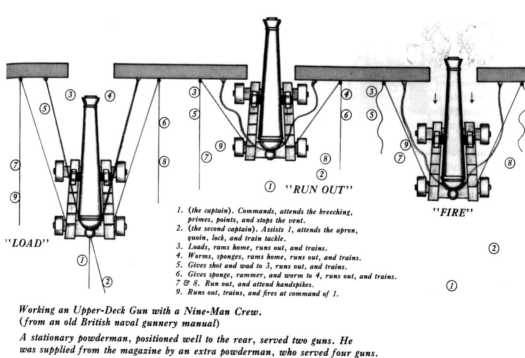

"LOAD" ① "RUN OUT" "FIRE"

1. (the captain). Commands, attends the breeching, primes, points, and stops the vent.
2. (the second captain). Assists 1, attends the apron, quoin, lock, and train tackle.
3. Loads, rams home, runs out, and trains.
4. Worms, sponges, rams home, runs out, and trains.
5. Gives shot and wad to 3, runs out, and trains.
6. Gives sponge, rammer, and worm to 4, runs out, and trains.
7 & 8. Run out, and attend handspikes.
9. Runs out, trains, and fires at command of 1.

Working an Upper-Deck Gun with a Nine-Man Crew.
(from an old British naval gunnery manual)

A stationary powderman, positioned well to the rear, served two guns. He was supplied from the magazine by an extra powderman, who served four guns.

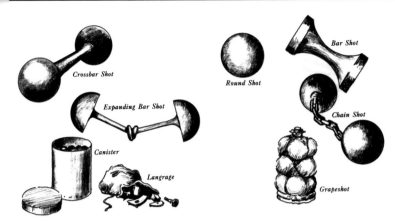

Types of shot fired by naval vessels of the period.

men, was responsible for loading, firing, and manhandling the cannon into position. Each man in the gun crew performed several tasks before the gun could be fired. The first step in reloading a gun was to "sponge," neutralizing any trace of burning cartridge from the previous volley and preventing the premature igniting of the next cartridge. One member of the gun crew would ram the wetted sponge, usually made of sheepskin, down to the bottom of the chamber, twist it around, draw it out, and then hit it against the outside of the muzzle of the gun to shake off any sparks or cartridge scraps that may have been picked up. The other end of the sponge was a rammer. A second member of the gun crew then rammed a cartridge down the gun chamber. This was followed by shot and then a wad to hold the ball in place. Every third time the gun was fired, a member of the gun crew would "worm" the gun. Using a corkscrew-like utensil, the sailor would draw out any pieces of the cartridge or wad that might have remained in the barrel after sponging.

After these operations were completed, other members of the gun crew pulled the gun back into firing position using side tackles hooked to rings on either side of the gun carriage and to the ship's sides. After each shot, the gun recoiled to the length of its breeching, a heavy rope running from a ring in the vessel's side through rings on either side of the carriage and through a ring lashed to or actually cast as part of the cascabel or small projection extending from the rear of the gun. The breeching allowed the guns to recoil far enough so that their muzzles ended up just inside the ship's hull and were thus accessible for loading. To adjust the elevation of a gun, the quoin, or graduated wedge, was moved in or out. To adjust the azimuth, or sideways direction of the firing, the gun crew used large wooden levers called handspikes and literally muscled the guns into the desired position. Predictably, the

adjustments that could be made under such conditions were crude.

After these operations were completed, the gun captain took a small iron skewer called a priming iron and thrust it down the small touchhole at the closed end of the gun tube and punctured the cartridge. Taking a priming tube, usually a length of quill filled with fine powder mixed with spirits of wine, he inserted it into the vent. Next he primed the vent using powder from a powder horn and lit that powder using a slow match, which was a cotton wick soaked in lye or another substance and twisted around a forked stick some three feet long. When the slow match touched the vent, there was a poof of flame and smoke, followed soon afterward by the flash and roar of the gun as the cartridge ignited. During this operation, the entire crew moved to the side of the gun so that the recoil would not crush them.

Firing three times in six minutes was considered a good rate of fire. Ideally, this meant that a ship of war could send a full broadside into the enemy ship every two minutes. Realistically, however, the speed of gun crews varied and as casualties began to mount, the firing became much less coordinated and more ragged.

Given the close ranges at which vessels fought, often less than one hundred yards, and with a fair rate of fire, one would expect that ships would have been quickly sunk. Actually, the size of the shot meant that only comparatively small holes could be punched in the hull and these could often be plugged from the inside. Also the motion of the hull thanks to the pitch of the sea, the crude method of elevating and depressing the guns, the great amounts of smoke that usually obscured the target, and the desire to fire quickly before the threatening gun muzzle opposite you could respond, meant that many shots missed their targets. As a result, ships during this time rarely sank in battle. Also, customarily the captain surrendered when things began to look hopeless.

Ships did, however, absorb great punishment. As the balls hit the wooden hulls, they would send splinters flying. These splinters inflicted terrible wounds among the crew. The phrase "the decks were awash with blood" was not an exaggeration. Also, if a ship launched a broadside through its opponent's bow or stern, which lacked the stout timbers found elsewhere, it could be devastating. There are instances in which half a crew was killed when their vessel was hit with such a raking broadside.

days up." Serving in the new Continental Navy would allow him to fulfill that childhood dream. Jones also professed a loftier motive for enlisting in the Patriot cause. He later wrote that he, though not an American but a "Citizen of the World," had joined up out of a love of liberty, a concern for "the Violated rights of Mankind," and a sense of "universal philanthropy." Jones has provided ample proof of being a romantic and an idealist; fighting to establish the right of a people to decide their destiny freely without coercion from a despotic king or his corrupt underlings appealed to these impulses.

Upon enrolling in the American cause, Jones was commissioned a lieutenant—the "Eldest" or most senior lieutenant in the navy. Jones could have commanded the sloop *Providence* but chose instead to serve as a lieutenant in the flagship of the commander in chief of the Continental Navy, Esek Hopkins, because, Jones said, his "highest Ambition" was to learn from a "Gentleman of Superiour Abilities[,] of superiour Merit." Jones believed he could be immediately useful and learn more seamanship and fleet maneuver by serving as a first lieutenant on *Alfred* than by commanding his own ship. He evidenced this same desire to increase his professional knowledge twice more: in 1778 when he requested that his friend, French fleet commander Lieutenant-General le Comte d'Orvilliers, allow him to go on board d'Orvilliers' flagship when the French sailed to attack a British flotilla protecting the English Channel; and in 1782 when he sailed as an observer on a French fleet going to the West Indies. In both cases, Jones hoped to study French battle tactics and fleet maneuvering in person. Throughout his career, Jones made learning and acquiring professional knowledge a priority.

In later years, Jones regretted his decision to sail in *Alfred* instead of accepting an independent command. Ever ambitious, Jones decided that a captaincy, even of a small vessel, would have established his

Portrait of John Paul Jones as a Continental Navy lieutenant.

seniority in the Navy and given him an opportunity of distinguishing himself. The outcome of the first operation involving *Alfred* heightened his dissatisfaction. Under the command of Hopkins, the fleet in 1777 captured the island of New Providence in the Bahamas. They captured the virtually undefended island easily; however, the governor in surrendering bought enough time to send away two hundred barrels of gunpowder, the capture of which had been the chief object of the expedition. On its way back from the Bahamas, the fleet sailed to Block Island, Rhode Island, hoping to capture British merchant vessels. While in those waters, it encountered the British warship HMS *Glasgow*, which should have been easy prey. The American attack was not well coordinated, however, and *Glasgow* escaped after mauling the American brig *Cabot*. Hopkins' conduct in the encounter with *Glasgow* convinced Jones that he had nothing to learn from the American commander in chief so that when he was again offered the command of *Providence* in the shuffling of positions that followed the *Glasgow* affair, Jones quickly accepted.

Independent Command

In August 1776, Jones set sail on his first independent cruise as captain of *Providence*. Operating as a commerce raider on this and a subsequent voyage, Jones enjoyed spectacular success. During his first voyage—off the Grand Banks—he captured sixteen prizes and destroyed the local fishing fleets. In his second cruise—again to the Grand Banks—he took several more prizes, including the armed transport *Mellish* with its cargo of winter uniforms, which were distributed to the nearly naked Continental Army. As he wrote his friend Joseph Hewes, a delegate to Congress from North Carolina: "In the term of Twelve weeks, including the time of fitting out . . . I took twenty four Prizes."

Anticipating that these successes would get him promoted to squadron commander, Jones was bitterly disappointed to discover that Congress had placed him 18th on the seniority list. One of Jones' failings as a naval officer and as a human being was his inability to distance himself from decisions that involved him or his career. Instead of appreciating that Congress was forced to appoint many of the men because they were well known in a particular geographical area and could therefore generate support to construct and man vessels for the navy, Jones interpreted his ranking as a slight on his honor and abilities. He should have understood that despite his being a foreigner with no natural political constituency or supporters, he still ranked high on the list of senior officers. Instead, he lashed out against some of those ranked above him in a series of intemperate letters. In a letter to Robert Morris, a Pennsylvania delegate to Congress and a member of the Marine Committee, Jones charged that several of the officers promoted over him were "altogether illiterate and Utterly ignorant of Marine Affairs." In another letter, Jones argued the new rankings slighted "the Gentleman or Man of Merit," by which Jones meant himself.

Esek Hopkins, Commander in Chief of the Continental Navy and Jones' first commander.

Going then from the purely personal to important ideas on the naval service in general—something Jones often did in such letters—he wrote "none other than a Gentleman, as well as a Seaman both in Theory and in Practise is qualified to support the Character of a Commission Officer in the Navy, nor is any Man fit to command a Ship of War, who is not also capable of communicating his Ideas on Paper in Language that becomes his Rank." Thus, Jones advo-

cated that the Marine Committee consider a candidate's character and communication skills as much as technical expertise in promoting an officer to command a ship or a fleet.

On another occasion, Jones suggested that the system of establishing seniority be based on merit. He proposed that commissioners, aided by "three or more of the most Judicious commanders of the Fleet," be appointed "to examine the abilities of Men who apply for Commissions, and make report to the Board [of Admiralty], also to examine divers Persons who now bear Commissions in the Service, and whoe's Abilities and accomplishments are very suspicious and uncertain." Jones therefore advocated a system of promotion based on merit rather than political influence or nepotism, a farsighted reform that would be long in coming. A system of merit promotion was particularly important for the naval service because "the Abilities of Sea Officers ought to be as far Superiour to the abilities of Officers in the Army as the nature of a Sea Service is more complicated, and admits of a greater number of Cases than can possibly happen on the Land—therefore the discipline by Sea ought to be the more perfect and regular." To this end, Jones came to advocate a training regimen for naval personnel that included schools for officers in the fleet and naval academies on shore. Although intemperate in some of

Continental Navy ship Alfred, *commanded by Jones, and Continental Navy sloop* Providence *capture the British armed transport* Mellish *and another British vessel.*

what he wrote, Jones was enough of a patriot to say in his letters that he could not "think of quiting the Service" while "the liberties of America are Unconfirmed."

In 1777, while pressing his case for advancement, Jones advocated a new naval strategy that demonstrates imagination, initiative, and audacity. Recognizing that the American navy was not strong enough to protect the country's coasts and that preying on British commercial shipping brought minimal strategic advantage because privateers did this task equally well, he and his patron Robert Morris advocated a different role for the small, young American navy. As Morris stated in a letter to Jones, they believed that the Navy's mission should be to "attack the Enemies defenceless places & there-

Model of the Continental Navy sloop-of-war Ranger, *which Jones commanded in 1777–1778.*

by oblige them to Station more of their Ships in their own Countries or to keep them employed in following ours and either way we are relieved so far as they do it." In other words, the Navy should hit the British where they least expected it and where they were most vulnerable. This strategy was, in fact, an extension of some of Lambert Wickes' ideas. Jones first suggested executing this strategy by leading a flotilla to Africa to prey on the "English African Trade which would not soon be recovered by not leaving them a Mast Standing on that Coast." Speaking for Congress, Robert Morris endorsed the main outlines of Jones' plan, but ordered that the attack be against British posts in the Caribbean, West Florida, and near the mouth of the Mississippi River instead.

The expedition never took place however. Jones blamed the jealousy and backwardness of the commander of the Continental Navy, Esek Hopkins; Hopkins cited the inability of the Navy to recruit men enough to man the ships needed for the proposed expedition. Instead, Jones was given command of *Ranger*, a sloop of war under construction at Portsmouth, New Hampshire, and was ordered to Europe. As it turned out, this appointment gave Jones the perfect opportunity to execute his plan of an attack on the British where they least expected it.

Taking the War to the Enemy's Shores

Before that could happen, however, Jones had to spend several months readying *Ranger* for sea. To Joseph Hewes, he explained that he and his officers had used "application and Industry" to scrounge the necessary "materials" to outfit the vessel. Despite their efforts, it was not until the end of October, some four months after command of the vessel had been given to Jones, that "a single suite of sails" was obtained. Jones commented that outfitting this "small ship" had given

him "more trouble" and cost him "more anxiety and Uneasiness than all the other duty which" he had "performed in the service."

As well as being a talented scrounger, Jones had a real technical understanding of ships and took great pains to maximize the performance of those he commanded. In the case of *Ranger*, he decided that the vessel was too lightly built to carry twenty cannon and reduced its armament to a more manageable eighteen guns. In so doing, he lowered the center of gravity for

Jones' ship Ranger *receiving the first recognition of the American flag by a foreign government.*

test, Jones ordered further alterations to the vessel in March 1778 hoping to improve its ability to sail to windward. Carpenters set the masts farther aft, sail-makers shortened the sails on the lower spars, and the crew repositioned the ballast. Finally, he had his crew scrape and clean the vessel's bottom, maximizing its speed. As evidenced here, Jones' success as a ship captain was the result of pre-campaign preparation as well as tactical decisions made in the heat of battle.

In the midst of these preparations, *Ranger* had gained the distinction of being the first vessel flying the Stars and Stripes to receive formal recognition from a foreign navy, thanks to Jones' efforts. On 13 February 1778 Jones anchored at Quiberon Bay where a squadron of line-of-battle ships and three frigates under the command of French Admiral La Motte Piquet were sitting at anchor waiting to escort an American-bound convoy away from the European coast. La Motte Piquet's presence gave Jones the opportunity he had long coveted to exchange salutes with a French flag officer. Jones sent a note saying that he was prepared to discharge a thirteen-gun salute if La Motte Piquet would "Return Gun for Gun." Jones was insulted when the French admiral replied that he would return the thirteen-gun salute with nine guns, but Jones was mollified on learning that nine guns was the same salute that was offered to "an Admiral of Holland or of any other Republic." He also saw it as an important symbolic moment because the salute was "an Acknowlidgement of American Independence."

At about the same time, Jones received orders from Benjamin Franklin, Silas Deane, and Arthur Lee, the American commissioners in France. Jones had sailed to Europe in anticipation that he would receive a frigate, *L'Indien*, which the American government had arranged to build in Holland. However, the British, learning of American plans, had persuaded the Dutch, in whose shipyard the vessel was being constructed, not to deliver *L'Indien* into American hands. The American commissioners, who were in the midst

the vessel. He also believed the vessel was over-sparred, a judgment confirmed by his voyage to France during which *Ranger* sailed "very Crank." To correct the defect, Jones made additional alterations in his vessel. He shortened the spars, added thirty tons of lead to the original ballast, and recut the sails. As a test voyage, he took *Ranger* into the rough winds and waters between Quiberon Bay and Brest, France. After the

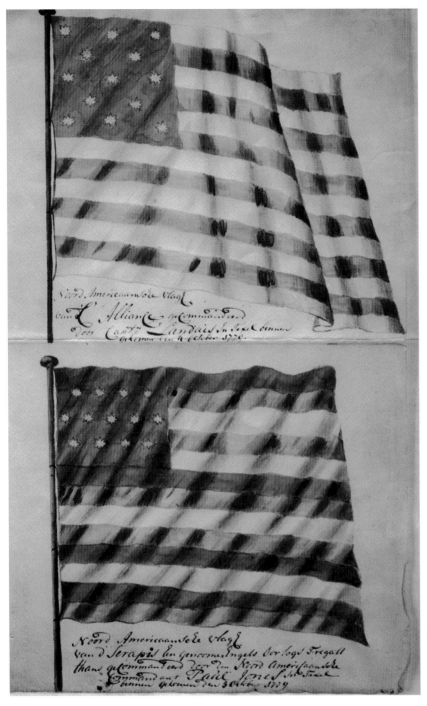

that small Squadrons could be employed to far better Advantage on private expeditions and would distress the Enemy infinitely more than the same force could do by cruising either Jointly or Seperately—were strict Secrecy Observed on our part the Enemy have many important Places in such a defenceless Situation that they might be effectually Surprised and Attacked with no considerable Force— We cannot yet Fight their Navy as their numbers and Force is so far Superiour to ours—therefore it seems to be our most natural Province to *Surprize* their defenceless places and thereby divide their attention and draw it off from our Coasts." In a February 1778 letter to the commissioners, Jones reiterated his ideas, adding: "I have in contemplation several enterprizes of some importance—the Commissioners do not even promise to Justify me should I fail in any bold attempt—I will not however, under this discouragement, alter my designs.—When an Enemy think a design against them improbable they can always be Surprised and Attacked with Advantage.—it is true I must run great risque—but no Gallant action was ever performed without danger— therefore, tho' I cannot insure Success I will endeavour to deserve it."

As seen in these two letters, Jones understood that Americans must fight a kind of guerilla war at sea. They could not engage the enemy fleet against fleet, nor was commerce raiding the answer. While the latter might be profitable for the captains and crews, it did not, in the end, significantly help the nation's interest. Striking the enemy where least expected would keep the

The flags flown by Jones on Alliance *and* Bonhomme Richard. *Right, John Paul Jones' cruises in European waters.*

of delicate negotiations with the French, decided not to press the matter. As a result, Jones was ordered to retain command of *Ranger* and, in that vessel, to attack the enemy. The orders the commissioners gave him, though vague, directed Jones to pursue the strategy he had advocated. He was to assault the enemy "by Sea, or otherwise." An earlier letter from Jones to the commissioners had spelled out his intentions: "I have always since we have had Ships of War been persuaded

British off-balance and dispersed, forcing them to redeploy some of their naval squadrons away from the American coast. Jones' ideas were "out of the box," and reflected a patriotism that was willing to sacrifice personal gain and advancement for a greater good. It was not, however, a strategy that appealed to his crew who saw commerce raiding and attendant prize money as their best chance to supplement meager wages. In *Ranger* and in his subsequent commands, Jones had

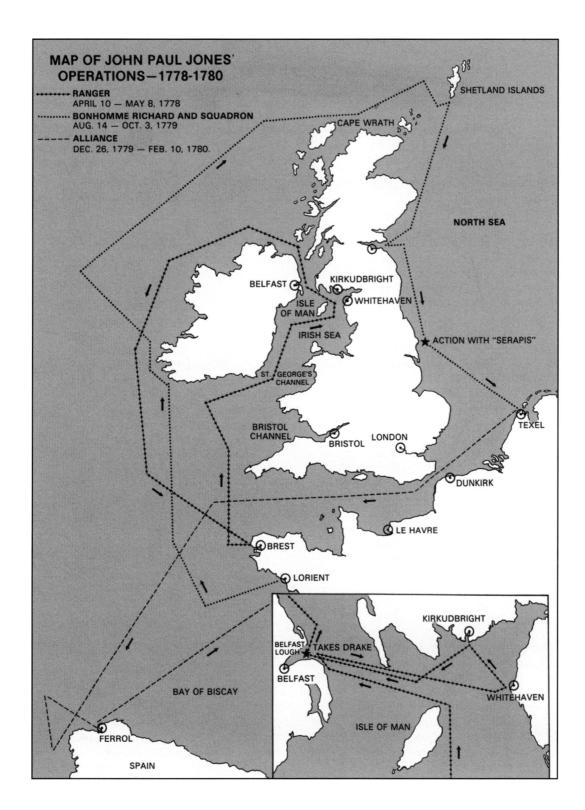

MAP OF JOHN PAUL JONES' OPERATIONS—1778-1780

•••••→ RANGER
APRIL 10 — MAY 8, 1778
••••••• BONHOMME RICHARD AND SQUADRON
AUG. 14 — OCT. 3, 1779
– – – – ALLIANCE
DEC. 26, 1779 — FEB. 10, 1780.

SHETLAND ISLANDS

CAPE WRATH

NORTH SEA

BELFAST
KIRKUDBRIGHT
WHITEHAVEN
ISLE OF MAN
IRISH SEA
ACTION WITH "SERAPIS"

ST. GEORGE'S CHANNEL

TEXEL

BRISTOL CHANNEL
BRISTOL
LONDON

DUNKIRK

LE HAVRE

BREST

LORIENT

BAY OF BISCAY

FERROL

SPAIN

KIRKUDBRIGHT

BELFAST LOUGH   TAKES DRAKE
BELFAST
WHITEHAVEN

ISLE OF MAN

problems with dissatisfied crews because of his reputation as a risk-taker and hard-fighter who eschewed commerce raiding for other, more perilous, missions.

The Cruise of Ranger

The cruise of *Ranger*, which began in April 1778, was truly remarkable. It lasted twenty-eight days, and in that time, according to historian Samuel Eliot Morison, Jones and his crew "performed one of the most brilliant exploits of the naval war." In addition to taking two merchantmen—Jones favored capturing merchant ships when it did not detract from the overall strategic goal   and destroying several others, *Ranger* captured a British man-of-war, took some two hundred prisoners, and, most notably, executed a land

raid that caught the public's attention in both England and America.

Jones had planned to raid a British coastal town as retaliation for English raids against towns on the Connecticut coast and in order to seize one or more "important" prisoners who might be exchanged for American seamen held in British prisons. The British government was willing to exchange captured American army officers and soldiers, but insisted on treating American naval prisoners as pirates who had no rights as belligerents. As a result, captured American seamen languished in British jails. The British could follow such a policy because American ships, especially privateers, captured few British pris-

Battle between Continental sloop-of-war *Ranger* and HMS *Drake*.

oners and kept even fewer. Concerned about the fate of these American naval prison- ers, Jones hoped that by taking an important English nobleman captive, he would force the British ministry to authorize an exchange. Jones mistakenly supposed that Lord Selkirk, his intended target, was a great lord whose detention would force the British to change their policy. Selkirk was, in fact, an unimportant Scottish peer. Moreover, he was away from home when Jones' raiding party arrived. Because of this, Jones—at the insistence of his crew—did noth- ing more than authorize his men to loot the Selkirk

Capture of Drake *by* Ranger.

household silver. Jones refused to accompany his men on their mission and later purchased the silver from his men and returned it to the Selkirks. He also wrote a lengthy, apologetic letter to Lady Selkirk spelling out the rationale for the raid.

This raid roused the countryside and caused the Admiralty to send warships in pursuit of *Ranger*. Jones, unaware that he was being chased, decided to attack the 20-gun British ship *Drake*. It was an even match. *Ranger* had more and heavier armament but *Drake* had more men. In contrast to his tactics at Flamborough Head, Jones decided to disable *Drake* with cannon fire while preventing the British warship from closing with *Ranger* and boarding it. In a battle that lasted just over an hour and was "warm close and obstinate," *Ranger* forced *Drake* to surrender. Jones, understanding the publicity value of bringing the British warship into a French port after his daring land raid, decided to take *Drake*, whose rigging was in tatters, with him to France. For almost twenty-four hours, therefore, he remained off Whitehaven, England, refitting the damaged *Drake*. He then sailed for France via the northern tip of Ireland, an inspired choice because his British pursuers had taken up a position south and east of Whitehaven on the more direct route to the continent.

Reaction to the raid in England is interesting. In some publications, Jones was characterized as a bloodthirsty pirate interested only in murder and mayhem. These newspaper accounts even changed his physical appearance, describing Jones, who was approximately 5'6", with light brown hair, fair skin, and hazel eyes, as big, dark and swarthy, like a buccaneer. (See illustration on page 65.) Despite the attempt to demonize Jones, many among the English lower classes came to see him as a Robin Hood figure, who took from the upper classes but was considerate of the English working man. This impression was solidified when on his return voyage to France Jones set ashore fishermen he had earlier captured to gain knowledge of the local waters and reportedly gave them new sails and money.

Heroism and Fame

With his success in *Ranger*, Jones gained command of a squadron, returning to British waters and fighting the battle off Flamborough Head. After that battle, Jones again eluded British patrol ships and with his

Cap.ᵗ Paul Jones,

From an Original Drawing taken from the Life, on board the Serapis.

London, Pub.ᵈ Oct.ᵣ 22, 1779, by Tho.ˢ Macklin, N.ᵒ 1, Lincolns Inn Fields.

John Paul Jones portrayed as a pirate.

squadron sailed into the Texel, Holland, on 3 October. While the battle was the pinnacle of Jones' naval career, in the period after the battle Jones demonstrated his shortcomings. He had always been concerned with his reputation, later asserting: "I have never served but for honor, I have never sought but glory." The victory over *Serapis* had given Jones that glory and he reveled in it to the point of neglecting his command and his crew. Shortly after arriving in the Texel, Jones traveled to Amsterdam where he was received as a hero and he played to that adulation. According to one of his midshipmen, Nathaniel Fanning, Jones "was treated as a conqueror. This so elated him with pride, that he had the vanity to go into the state house, mount the balcony or piazza, and shew himself in the front thereof, to the populace and people of distinction then walking on the public parade." Jones also

worked as his own publicist to further his fame.

During October and November, Jones wrote dozens of letters, gave interviews, and helped to get accounts of the battle published widely in European newspapers. This publicity was not without benefit because it helped further the American cause. The problem was that Jones focused on it to the detriment of his command. As a friend and American agent in the Netherlands warned him in a letter of 18 October: "I have seen persons of authority here who are warm friends of America and who have spoken to me much about your squadron. Their opinion is that you did not do wrong to come and show yourself here; but, on the other hand, they think that you should not repeat this step, because that would give you too much publicity and it would produce a bad effect. . . . I must warn you also, my dear sir, that these same friends told me something which, whether or not it is true, hurts me as much as it does them, namely that, according to what one says, there reigns a great filth and infection in the *Serapis*; people have seen pieces of cadavers left from the battle. . . . This shocks people here right now and makes one fear the consequences of such negligence. In the name of God, my dear sir, put order in all this. Do not leave your ship again. Have it cleaned and purged of this filth."

Jones' quest for fame also led him to diminish unfairly the contributions made by fellow officers during the engagement with *Serapis*. One of the captains in Jones' squadron, Denis-Nicholas Cottineau, whom Jones considered a friend, wrote a memoir that was highly critical of Jones when he became irritated with his insufferable self-promotion. As Cottineau wrote on 15 November 1779: "Ungrateful to his crew, he makes it seem that he alone did everything." Nor was this a new

John Paul Jones, a heroic figure to ordinary sailors such as the one who carved this scrimshaw portrait of him.

development. Throughout his service in the Continental Navy, Jones was slow to credit subordinates or superiors and quick to criticize them. As a result, he comes across as ungrateful, super-sensitive, and self-absorbed.

Another incident, the "mutiny" of the crew of *Alliance*, which occurred in June 1780, also had its origins in Jones' self-absorption. Although Jones wanted to refit and sail *Serapis*, pressure from the English government on the still-neutral government of the Netherlands forced Jones to turn that vessel over to the French before the Dutch government could seize it and return it to the English. Jones then took command of the frigate *Alliance* and slipped out of the Texel, eluding a blockading English squadron. He first took *Alliance* to Spain and then to Lorient, France, to refit. While *Alliance* was at Lorient, Jones traveled to Paris and again began a campaign of self-promotion that culminated in his being awarded the Order of Military Merit and a gold sword by King Louis XVI. While Jones was gone, Pierre Landais, the

Continental Navy frigate Alliance, *whose crew "mutinied" and abandoned Jones in France, by Matthew Parke, a Marine officer who served with Jones.*

former commander of *Alliance* whom Jones had charged with treachery at the battle of Flamborough Head, boarded *Alliance* and convinced the crew that Jones was trying to rob them of prize money and that he, Landais, was their only hope for returning to America. With Landais in command, *Alliance* sailed from Lorient for the United States despite efforts by Jones to stop them.

Jones blamed the port officials at Lorient for not doing more to thwart Landais, but a letter from Benjamin Franklin, the American minister to France and Jones' patron and friend, is quite revealing. Franklin wrote: "If you had stayed on board where your duty lay, instead of coming to Paris, you would not have lost your ship. Now you blame them [the port officers] as having deserted you in recovering her; though relinquishing to prevent mischief was a voluntary act of your own, for which you have credit; hereafter, if you should observe an occasion to give your officers and friends a little more praise than is their due, and confess more fault than you can justly be charged with, you will only become the sooner for it, a great captain. Criticizing and censuring almost every one you have to do with, will diminish friends, increase enemies, and thereby hurt your affairs."

Having lost *Alliance*, Jones was given command of *Ariel*, a corvette built for the British navy but seized by the French and lent to the United States to carry supplies to America. On taking command of it, however, Jones, always interested in ship design and performance, decided that the vessel needed to be rerigged to improve its sailing abilities and further delayed his departure to America. Almost as soon as *Ariel* left Lorient in September 1779, it was caught in a vicious gale that battered the French coast and destroyed numerous ships. *Ariel* survived—thanks to Jones' superior seamanship—but lost two masts and had to return to Lorient for repairs, keeping Jones and the vessel in France until February 1781.

Jones seems to have anticipated that he would be received as a hero when he arrived in America. Instead he was met with a congressional investigation. Certain delegates, hoping to use Jones' conduct in France as a means to discredit Franklin, initiated an investigation into the question of whether Jones had unnecessarily delayed the shipment of war supplies to America. Quickly deciding that the investigation would not achieve what they had hoped, these delegates abandoned the inquiry and turned the matter over to the Board of Admiralty. The secretary of the board submitted forty-seven questions to Jones, who, as a master of self-promotion, skillfully answered, highlighting his triumphs and blaming any problems on others, most notably Pierre Landais. Jones' triumph was confirmed when the French ambassador conferred on Jones the Order du Mérite Militaire, the highest award that the French could give to a foreigner. Congress then voted a resolution of thanks to Jones and gave him command of *America*, the Continental Navy's only ship of the line, which was then being built at Portsmouth, New Hampshire.

Jones hoped to use *America* as the flagship of a flotilla that would once again attack England, but on arriving at Portsmouth to oversee its completion and launch, he was surprised to find progress on the vessel so "backward." While Jones actively supervised construction and the procurement of craftsmen and materials needed to complete the vessel, inadequate funds from the near-bankrupt Continental government meant that work on *America* progressed sporadically and slowly. In the end, a cash-strapped Congress presented *America* to the French as a replacement for a French man-of-war that had been destroyed on a sandbar outside of Boston Harbor.

The Final Years

The failure to complete *America* in time for active duty and the intrigue of other Continental captains denied Jones his fondest dream, a rear admiral's rank in the Continental Navy. The remaining years of Jones' life were spent trying to increase his professional knowledge of fleet command and to convince Congress that he should be appointed the United States Navy's first admiral. Such actions included his obtaining permission to accompany a French fleet to the West Indies in 1782-1783 to study fleet evolutions. While on that cruise, Jones became so ill that when he returned to America in May 1783, Robert Morris believed that he would die. After his recovery, he sought and received permission to travel to Europe, ostensibly to recover prize money owed to the officers and men of *Bonhomme Richard* and to serve as a reminder of the American navy in European capitals. He again sought an admiral's commission to enhance his prestige, but this honor was denied him. The mission was successful and Jones returned to the United States in 1787. Presenting his accounts for the French prize money negotiations to Congress, he again sought to be named a rear admiral. While the title would have been an honorary one at best because the United States had no navy at the time, captains who were senior to him blocked the request.

Frustrated, Jones left the United States for France in 1788. He was sent ostensibly to obtain prize money, this time from Denmark. While in Denmark, he was offered a commission in the Imperial Russian Navy. Attracted by the opportunity to command a fleet and hoping that his new title would impress Congress enough to award him with an admiral's rank, and attracted by the prospect of adventure and glory, Jones accepted the offer and set out for St. Petersburg. Sent to the Black Sea, the new rear admiral believed he would command all the naval forces in that theater in their operations against the Turks, but quickly learned that three other rear admirals served in the command and each jealously guarded his powers and privileges. Jones was instrumental in the Russian navy victory at Liman, but another admiral, Prince Nassau-Siegen, a friend of Empress Catherine II's key advisor, Gregorii Aleksandrovich, Prince Potemkin, successfully usurped all the credit for the victory. Jones was recalled to Moscow and spent several months making plans until a trumped-up sex charge linking Jones and a young

John Paul Jones' crypt at the United States Naval Academy.

girl scandalized the empress and ended any chances for his restoration to command.

In the end, he returned to Paris where he remained without money and prospects, all but ignored until his death in July 1792 at the age of forty-five after months of suffering from jaundice and other diseases. Ironically, only days before his death, Jones had been named a commissioner to negotiate with the dey of Algiers concerning the release of American sailors held prisoner by the dey. Jones was buried in Paris and the site of his grave quickly forgotten. Only in 1905 was Jones' grave rediscovered. His remains were returned to the United States to be re-interred in a magnificent tomb at the United States Naval Academy.

While Jones was revered through much of the nineteenth century as a hero who exhibited dauntless courage and unconquerable persistence in the face of overwhelming odds, it was not until the twentieth

century that his professionalism and abilities as a "complete" naval officer came to be appreciated. His strategic vision that placed the nation's interest over his own personal gain, his rise to the top levels of the new American navy through dint of hard work and application, his skill as a naval architect, his continued study to better himself as an officer and commander, and his attempts to reform the Navy and to substitute merit and ability in place of nepotism and influence, all marked him as one who sought to professionalize the early Navy. While his personal shortcomings—his penchant for criticizing others, his inability to credit subordinates, self-promotion, and self-absorption—left him an outsider in the American naval service, he nonetheless became a symbol for the best that was to become the United States Navy and those who served in it.

Glossary

adventure: a speculation in goods sent abroad to be sold or bartered for profit (merchant sailors were customarily allowed to carry on board small amounts of goods on their own accounts)

brig: a two-masted, square-rigged vessel

brigantine: a two-masted, square-rigged vessel, differing from a brig in that it does not carry a square mainsail

broadside: (a) the simultaneous discharge of all the cannon on one side of a ship of war; (b) the weight of the shot fired by a single such discharge

carriage gun: a cannon set on a wheeled support

corvette: a ship-rigged warship, similar to, but smaller than, a frigate

crank: (a) having the quality of a vessel easily tipped by external force; (b) incapable of carrying sail without danger of capsizing

cutter: (a) a fore-and-aft-rigged, sharp-built vessel with a jib, forestaysail, mainsail, and single mast; (b) a medium-sized ship's boat

frigate: a ship-rigged, three-masted warship, with more than one sail per mast, carrying between twenty and forty-four guns on more than one deck

galley: a long vessel of war using both sails and oars

heave down: to place a vessel on its side for caulking or repairing; also called careen

heave to: to bring a vessel's head to the wind and adjust the sails so it will remain stationary, or nearly so

ketch: a small vessel rigged with two masts set nearly where the two after masts would be set in a three masted vessel, leaving a clear deck forward of the mainmast

letter of marque: (a) a commission issued by government licensing the commander of a privately owned ship to cruise in search of enemy merchant vessels; (b) a vessel bearing such a commission (more frequently called a privateer)

line of battle ship: see ship of the line

lugger: a small fishing or coasting vessel carrying lugsails, four-sided sails attached to a yard that hangs obliquely on a mast and is hoisted and lowered with the sail

mast: an upright spar rising from the keel or deck of a ship and supporting the yards, booms, and rigging

pendant: pennant, any of various nautical flags tapering to a point or swallowtail and used for identification or signaling

privateer: an armed private ship commissioned to cruise against the commerce or warships of an enemy

prize money: a part of the proceeds of a captured ship divided among the officers and men making the capture

quarter: the clemency of not killing a defeated enemy

quarters: (a) the stern area of a ship's sides; (b) assigned stations or posts.

royals: the fourth set of mast, sail, and yard above a vessel's deck

rigging: a general name for all ropes employed to support and work masts, yards, sails, and so forth

schooner: a fore-and-aft rigged vessel having two masts with a smaller sail on the foremast and with the mainmast stepped nearly amidships

ship of the line: a ship of war large enough to have a place in the line of battle (during the American Revolution, these ships carried a minimum of fifty guns on a minimum of two decks)

ship rig: the arrangement of a vessel carrying eleven or twelve square sails on three masts, extended by yards, and also a number of fore-and-aft sails

sloop: a fore-and-aft rigged vessel with one mast and a single headsail jib

sloop of war: a vessel of war next in size to a frigate

snow: the largest two-masted vessel of the period; usually served as a merchant vessel

spar: a stout rounded wood piece, as a mast, boom, gaff, or yard, used to support rigging

swivel gun: a small cannon fixed on a pivot

tack: (a) the direction of a ship with respect to the trim of the sails (a vessel is on the starboard tack when the wind blows against the starboard side, and on the port tack when the wind blows against the port side); (b) to change the direction of a vessel from one tack to another when close-hauled by bringing the head into the wind and causing it to fall off with the wind on the other bow, by using the helm and sails

wear: to put a ship on the other tack by turning the bow away from the wind